THE AVIATION WORKSHOP PUBLICATIONS LTD
ON-TARGET PROFILE N

GW00569814

The F-86 Sabr

in RAF, RCAF, RAAF, SAAF, PAF and ....

by Jon Freeman

The F-86 Sabre, is without a doubt a classic jet aircraft that saw front line service in all corners of the World, from Korea in the 1950s up until the mid-1970s. The air forces of the British Commonwealth were quick to see the potential of this sleek, swept wing fighter and both Canadiar in Canada and the Commonwealth Aircraft Corporation (CAC) in Australia, built the Sabre under license production. In the case of the CAC built machines, these involved major redesigns to suit RAAF requirements.

The Sabres used by the air forces covered in this Profile operated in many environments and wore many different colour schemes and markings. We have tried to show a wide variety of these schemes and hope to have illustrated a few that are not widely known or infrequently published. Many of the rare schemes have come to light due to the information from some private collections in Canada and Australia.

These On-Target Profiles are designed to compliment your existing camouflage and marking reference material. They are not designed to be the 'last word' on the subject, but act as a great source of inspiration - for aviation enthusiasts and modellers alike.

On-Target Profiles are produced by The Aviation Workshop as part of a package of products for the enthusiast and modeller, including two special Model Alliance Decal sheets in 1/72 and 1/48 scale, covering some of the Sabres illustrated in this book.

First Published in Great Britain in 2004 by
The Aviation Workshop Publications Ltd
& Gary Madgwick
Brook Barn, Letcombe Regis, Wantage,
Oxon, OX12 9JD, UK
Tel: 01235 769038 Fax: 01235 771432
Email: sales@theaviationworkshop.co.uk
Website: www.theaviationworkshop.co.uk

Copyright 2004
The Aviation Workshop Publications Ltd

Artwork and artwork captions by Jon Freeman
Edited by Gary Madgwick
Designed by The Aviation Workshop Publications Ltd
Additional information and text by Mark Rolfe and Gary Madgwick

Printed in England by PHPLitho Printers Ltd
Hoyle Mill, Barnsley,
South Yorkshire, S71 1HN

ISBN 1-904643-05-1

Distribution and Marketing in UK by
The Aviation Workshop Publications Ltd
Trade terms available on request

All enquires regarding this publication, past publications or future projects and publications should be directed to the publishers.

Canadian Roundels and Crests were used with permission of the Canadian Armed Forces and Canadian Government 2004.

Australian Roundels and badges are produced with the kind permission of the Australian Department of Defence 2004.

Royal Air Force, page 2

Royal Canadian Air Force
page 13

Royal Australian Air Force
page 28

South African Air Force
page 38

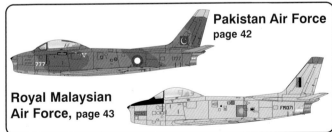

Pakistan Air Force
page 42

Royal Malaysian
Air Force, page 43

Publisher's Note
In preparing this book, we have always tried to work from colour photographs and to confirm markings and serial numbers from more than one source. In the few instances were photographs have not been available, great care has been taken to cross-reference all available data and research material and to this end the following books need mention:-
'**Canadiar and Commonwealth Sabre**' Warpaint No 40 by Steve Hazell, Published by Warpaint Books; '**The Canadiar Sabre**' by Larry Milbury, Published by CANAV Books; '**Modern Combat Aircraft, F-86 Sabre**' by Maurice Allward, Published by Ian Allan Books; '**A View of the North American (CAC) Sabre**' by John Hopton, Published by NASMA Books and '**Aircam No.20 - Canadair and Commonwealth Sabre**' by Richard Ward, Aircam Aviation Series.
Very special thanks are also due to:- Darren Mottram and Rod Farquar, Marc Brauyere, Gary Byk, Micheal Kirk, Mike McEvoy, Adrian Balch, Mark Rolfe, Paul Tuckey, Mike Burns and Dale Clark, without whose combined efforts, this book would have been much more difficult. Gary Madgwick, October 2004

Royal Air Force

At the beginning of the 1950s, the two principal jet-powered fighters in Royal Air Force service were the Gloster Meteor and the de Havilland Vampire, both of which were essentially 'first-generation jet' designs. The Supermarine Swift and Hawker Hunter were still in their development stages, although the former would ultimately turn out to be ill-suited to the home defence role anyway.

An agreement was reached between the British and US governments, whereby the United States would pay for the aircraft, which would be built under licence and supplied by Canadair Aircraft Ltd, under the Mutual Defence Assistance Program, (MDAP).

The first Canadair-built Sabres for the RAF, were three Mk 2s, delivered in the autumn of 1952 for pilot transition training over to the type, pending full delivery. In December of that year, the first batches of Canadair Sabre F Mk 4s were delivered.

This initial batch was finished in an overall natural metal scheme with red wingtips, (and sometimes, horizontal tail units), but this soon gave way to a much more business-like Dark Sea Grey and Dark Green upper surface scheme over PRU Blue or Silver undersides, applied by Maintenance Units, (MUs), in the UK.

During this time period, the Royal Air Force was starting to resurrect the colourful unit markings that had been so prevalent before World War Two, and the Sabre squadrons were amongst the RAF units to benefit from this situation.

A total of 428 Sabre F Mk 4s were delivered between December 1952 and December 1953, under a programme codenamed 'Beacher's Brook', after the famous jump at Aintree Racecourse.

The first RAF unit to receive the Sabre was No 67 Sqn, 2nd Tactical Air Force, in May 1953. Thereafter, Nos. 3, 4, 20, 26, 71, 93, 112, 130 and 234 Squadrons, all part of Royal Air Force Germany, (RAFG), were equipped with the type. Two United Kingdom-based units, Nos 66 and 92 Squadrons also operated Mk 4s for homeland defence, based at RAF Leconfield, together with No 229 OCU (Operational Conversion Unit), operating from RAF Chivenor. Although their RAF service was brief, the Sabre was reportedly well liked by its crews.

By mid-1956, all had been replaced by the Hawker Hunter. Ex-RAF aircraft were passed on to other air forces, such as Italy, Greece and Yugoslavia. Some ex-Yugoslavian machines eventually turned up in Honduras. One ex-RAF Sabre, serial number XB982, was passed on to Bristol-Siddeley, as a test bed for that company's Orpheus 801 jet engine. It was envisaged that this engine be used to power RAF Sabres, but by that time, the aircraft had reached the end of its RAF life, so the idea was not proceeded with.

Between 1956 and 1958, some 302 ex-RAF Sabres were passed on to the USAF and given spurious serial numbers, (these were actually the original Canadian serials), where they were given the designation F-86E(M) ('M' stood for 'modified'), and used in a number of non-operational roles.

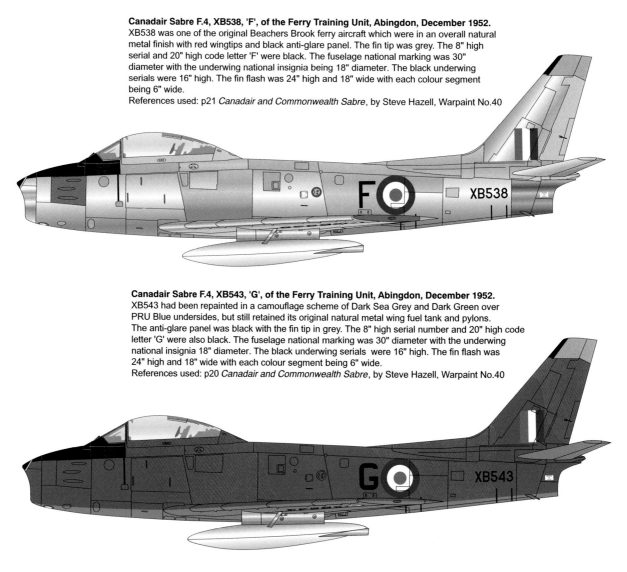

Canadair Sabre F.4, XB538, 'F', of the Ferry Training Unit, Abingdon, December 1952.
XB538 was one of the original Beachers Brook ferry aircraft which were in an overall natural metal finish with red wingtips and black anti-glare panel. The fin tip was grey. The 8" high serial and 20" high code letter 'F' were black. The fuselage national marking was 30" diameter with the underwing national insignia being 18" diameter. The black underwing serials were 16" high. The fin flash was 24" high and 18" wide with each colour segment being 6" wide.
References used: p21 *Canadair and Commonwealth Sabre*, by Steve Hazell, Warpaint No.40

Canadair Sabre F.4, XB543, 'G', of the Ferry Training Unit, Abingdon, December 1952.
XB543 had been repainted in a camouflage scheme of Dark Sea Grey and Dark Green over PRU Blue undersides, but still retained its original natural metal wing fuel tank and pylons. The anti-glare panel was black with the fin tip in grey. The 8" high serial number and 20" high code letter 'G' were also black. The fuselage national marking was 30" diameter with the underwing national insignia 18" diameter. The black underwing serials were 16" high. The fin flash was 24" high and 18" wide with each colour segment being 6" wide.
References used: p20 *Canadair and Commonwealth Sabre*, by Steve Hazell, Warpaint No.40

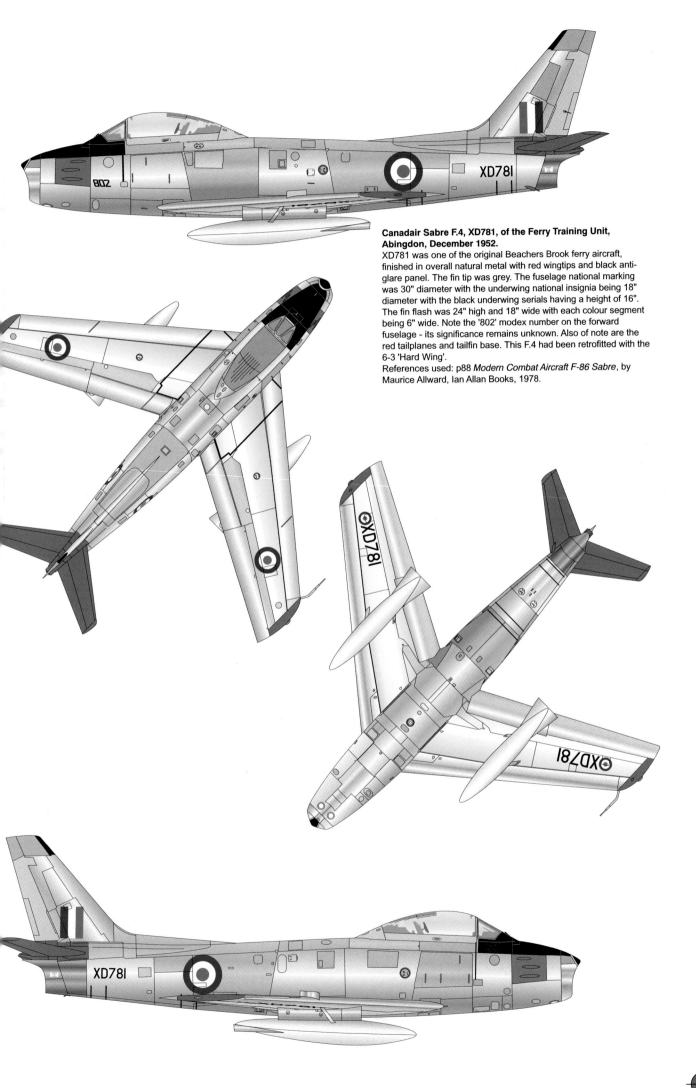

Canadair Sabre F.4, XD781, of the Ferry Training Unit, Abingdon, December 1952.
XD781 was one of the original Beachers Brook ferry aircraft, finished in overall natural metal with red wingtips and black anti-glare panel. The fin tip was grey. The fuselage national marking was 30" diameter with the underwing national insignia being 18" diameter with the black underwing serials having a height of 16". The fin flash was 24" high and 18" wide with each colour segment being 6" wide. Note the '802' modex number on the forward fuselage - its significance remains unknown. Also of note are the red tailplanes and tailfin base. This F.4 had been retrofitted with the 6-3 'Hard Wing'.
References used: p88 *Modern Combat Aircraft F-86 Sabre*, by Maurice Allward, Ian Allan Books, 1978.

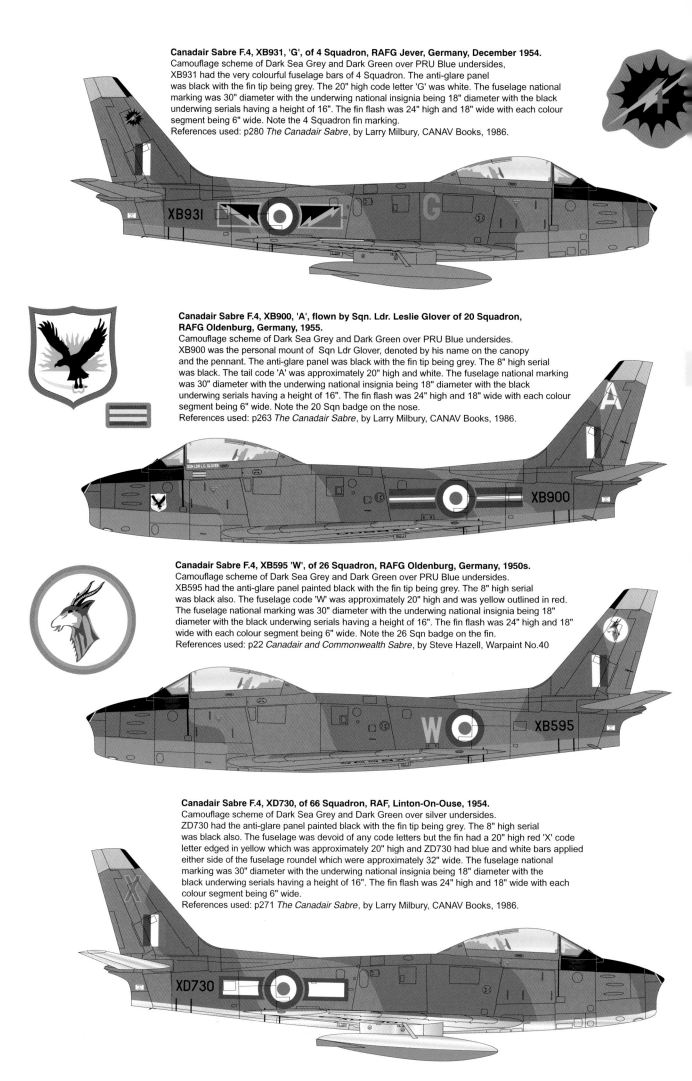

Canadair Sabre F.4, XB931, 'G', of 4 Squadron, RAFG Jever, Germany, December 1954.
Camouflage scheme of Dark Sea Grey and Dark Green over PRU Blue undersides,
XB931 had the very colourful fuselage bars of 4 Squadron. The anti-glare panel
was black with the fin tip being grey. The 20" high code letter 'G' was white. The fuselage national
marking was 30" diameter with the underwing national insignia being 18" diameter with the black
underwing serials having a height of 16". The fin flash was 24" high and 18" wide with each colour
segment being 6" wide. Note the 4 Squadron fin marking.
References used: p280 *The Canadair Sabre*, by Larry Milbury, CANAV Books, 1986.

**Canadair Sabre F.4, XB900, 'A', flown by Sqn. Ldr. Leslie Glover of 20 Squadron,
RAFG Oldenburg, Germany, 1955.**
Camouflage scheme of Dark Sea Grey and Dark Green over PRU Blue undersides.
XB900 was the personal mount of Sqn Ldr Glover, denoted by his name on the canopy
and the pennant. The anti-glare panel was black with the fin tip being grey. The 8" high serial
was black. The tail code 'A' was approximately 20" high and white. The fuselage national marking
was 30" diameter with the underwing national insignia being 18" diameter with the black
underwing serials having a height of 16". The fin flash was 24" high and 18" wide with each colour
segment being 6" wide. Note the 20 Sqn badge on the nose.
References used: p263 *The Canadair Sabre*, by Larry Milbury, CANAV Books, 1986.

Canadair Sabre F.4, XB595 'W', of 26 Squadron, RAFG Oldenburg, Germany, 1950s.
Camouflage scheme of Dark Sea Grey and Dark Green over PRU Blue undersides.
XB595 had the anti-glare panel painted black with the fin tip being grey. The 8" high serial
was black also. The fuselage code 'W' was approximately 20" high and was yellow outlined in red.
The fuselage national marking was 30" diameter with the underwing national insignia being 18"
diameter with the black underwing serials having a height of 16". The fin flash was 24" high and 18"
wide with each colour segment being 6" wide. Note the 26 Sqn badge on the fin.
References used: p22 *Canadair and Commonwealth Sabre*, by Steve Hazell, Warpaint No.40

Canadair Sabre F.4, XD730, of 66 Squadron, RAF, Linton-On-Ouse, 1954.
Camouflage scheme of Dark Sea Grey and Dark Green over silver undersides.
ZD730 had the anti-glare panel painted black with the fin tip being grey. The 8" high serial
was black also. The fuselage was devoid of any code letters but the fin had a 20" high red 'X' code
letter edged in yellow which was approximately 20" high and ZD730 had blue and white bars applied
either side of the fuselage roundel which were approximately 32" wide. The fuselage national
marking was 30" diameter with the underwing national insignia being 18" diameter with the
black underwing serials having a height of 16". The fin flash was 24" high and 18" wide with each
colour segment being 6" wide.
References used: p271 *The Canadair Sabre*, by Larry Milbury, CANAV Books, 1986.

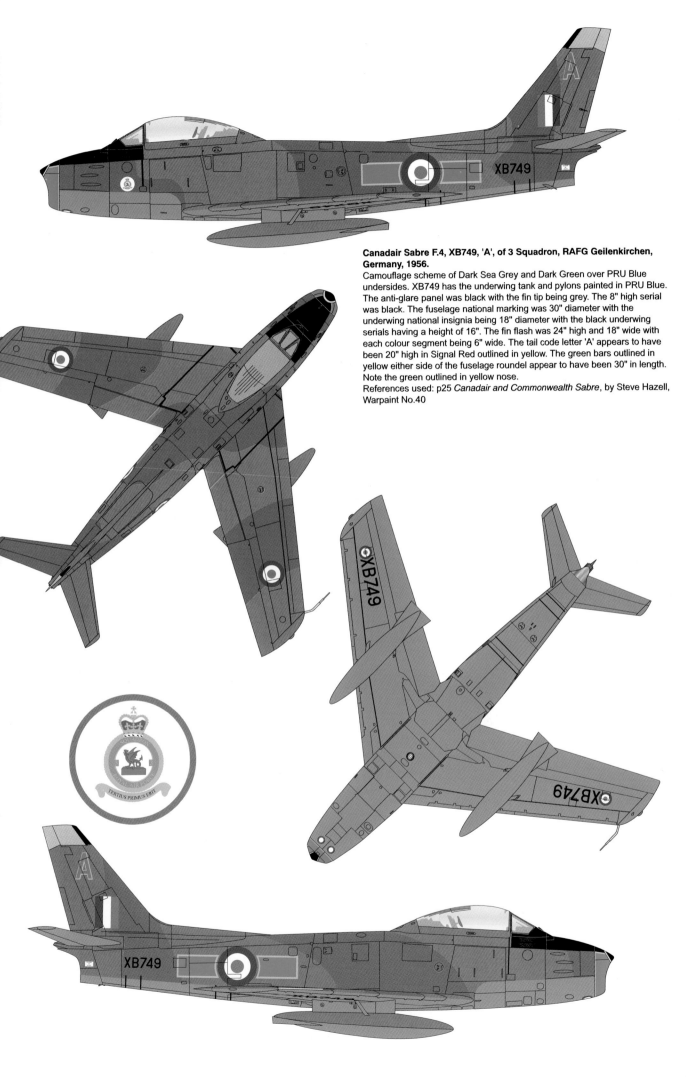

Canadair Sabre F.4, XB749, 'A', of 3 Squadron, RAFG Geilenkirchen, Germany, 1956.

Camouflage scheme of Dark Sea Grey and Dark Green over PRU Blue undersides. XB749 has the underwing tank and pylons painted in PRU Blue. The anti-glare panel was black with the fin tip being grey. The 8" high serial was black. The fuselage national marking was 30" diameter with the underwing national insignia being 18" diameter with the black underwing serials having a height of 16". The fin flash was 24" high and 18" wide with each colour segment being 6" wide. The tail code letter 'A' appears to have been 20" high in Signal Red outlined in yellow. The green bars outlined in yellow either side of the fuselage roundel appear to have been 30" in length. Note the green outlined in yellow nose.

References used: p25 *Canadair and Commonwealth Sabre*, by Steve Hazell, Warpaint No.40

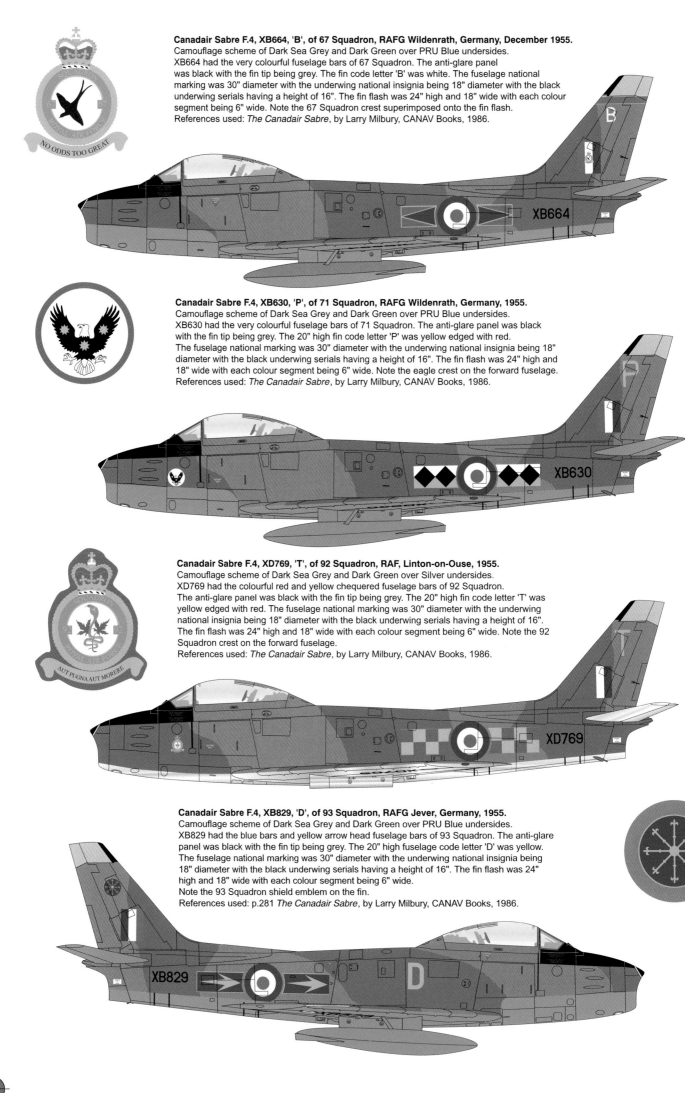

Canadair Sabre F.4, XB664, 'B', of 67 Squadron, RAFG Wildenrath, Germany, December 1955.
Camouflage scheme of Dark Sea Grey and Dark Green over PRU Blue undersides.
XB664 had the very colourful fuselage bars of 67 Squadron. The anti-glare panel
was black with the fin tip being grey. The fin code letter 'B' was white. The fuselage national
marking was 30" diameter with the underwing national insignia being 18" diameter with the black
underwing serials having a height of 16". The fin flash was 24" high and 18" wide with each colour
segment being 6" wide. Note the 67 Squadron crest superimposed onto the fin flash.
References used: *The Canadair Sabre*, by Larry Milbury, CANAV Books, 1986.

Canadair Sabre F.4, XB630, 'P', of 71 Squadron, RAFG Wildenrath, Germany, 1955.
Camouflage scheme of Dark Sea Grey and Dark Green over PRU Blue undersides.
XB630 had the very colourful fuselage bars of 71 Squadron. The anti-glare panel was black
with the fin tip being grey. The 20" high fin code letter 'P' was yellow edged with red.
The fuselage national marking was 30" diameter with the underwing national insignia being 18"
diameter with the black underwing serials having a height of 16". The fin flash was 24" high and
18" wide with each colour segment being 6" wide. Note the eagle crest on the forward fuselage.
References used: *The Canadair Sabre*, by Larry Milbury, CANAV Books, 1986.

Canadair Sabre F.4, XD769, 'T', of 92 Squadron, RAF, Linton-on-Ouse, 1955.
Camouflage scheme of Dark Sea Grey and Dark Green over Silver undersides.
XD769 had the colourful red and yellow chequered fuselage bars of 92 Squadron.
The anti-glare panel was black with the fin tip being grey. The 20" high fin code letter 'T' was
yellow edged with red. The fuselage national marking was 30" diameter with the underwing
national insignia being 18" diameter with the black underwing serials having a height of 16".
The fin flash was 24" high and 18" wide with each colour segment being 6" wide. Note the 92
Squadron crest on the forward fuselage.
References used: *The Canadair Sabre*, by Larry Milbury, CANAV Books, 1986.

Canadair Sabre F.4, XB829, 'D', of 93 Squadron, RAFG Jever, Germany, 1955.
Camouflage scheme of Dark Sea Grey and Dark Green over PRU Blue undersides.
XB829 had the blue bars and yellow arrow head fuselage bars of 93 Squadron. The anti-glare
panel was black with the fin tip being grey. The 20" high fuselage code letter 'D' was yellow.
The fuselage national marking was 30" diameter with the underwing national insignia being
18" diameter with the black underwing serials having a height of 16". The fin flash was 24"
high and 18" wide with each colour segment being 6" wide.
Note the 93 Squadron shield emblem on the fin.
References used: p.281 *The Canadair Sabre*, by Larry Milbury, CANAV Books, 1986.

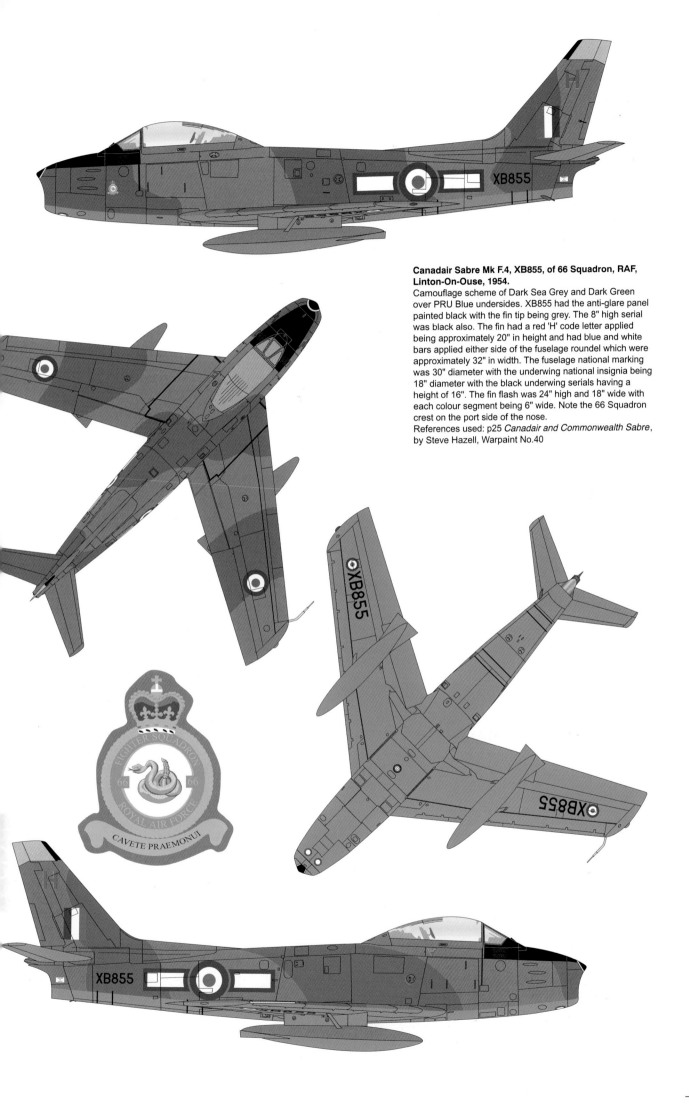

Canadair Sabre Mk F.4, XB855, of 66 Squadron, RAF, Linton-On-Ouse, 1954.
Camouflage scheme of Dark Sea Grey and Dark Green over PRU Blue undersides. XB855 had the anti-glare panel painted black with the fin tip being grey. The 8" high serial was black also. The fin had a red 'H' code letter applied being approximately 20" in height and had blue and white bars applied either side of the fuselage roundel which were approximately 32" in width. The fuselage national marking was 30" diameter with the underwing national insignia being 18" diameter with the black underwing serials having a height of 16". The fin flash was 24" high and 18" wide with each colour segment being 6" wide. Note the 66 Squadron crest on the port side of the nose.
References used: p25 *Canadair and Commonwealth Sabre*, by Steve Hazell, Warpaint No.40

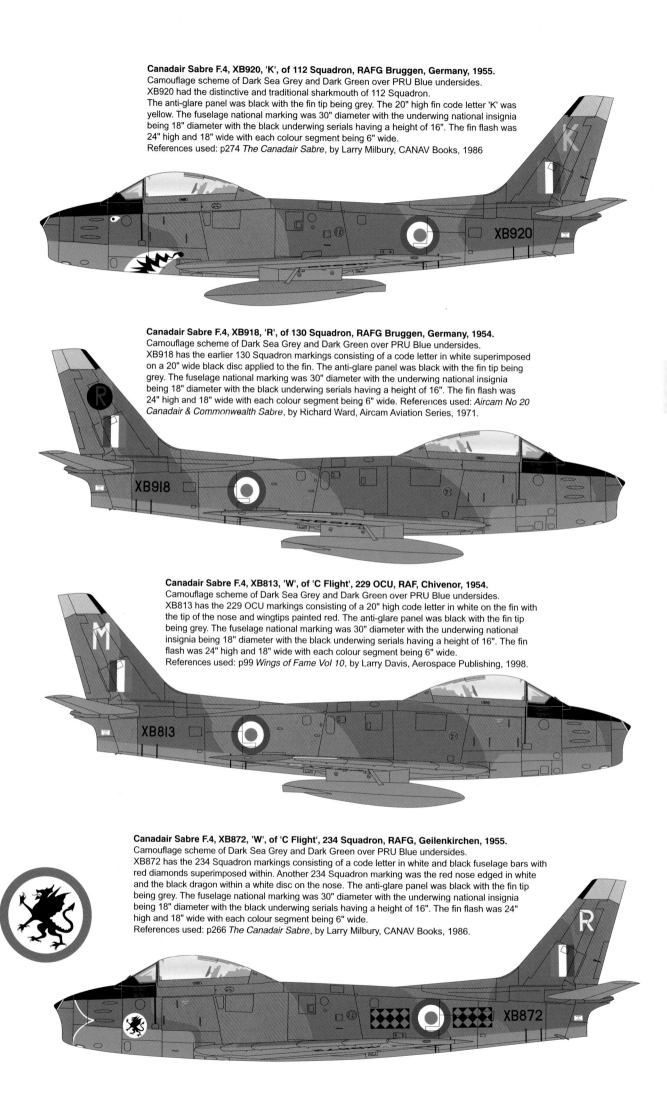

Canadair Sabre F.4, XB920, 'K', of 112 Squadron, RAFG Bruggen, Germany, 1955.
Camouflage scheme of Dark Sea Grey and Dark Green over PRU Blue undersides.
XB920 had the distinctive and traditional sharkmouth of 112 Squadron.
The anti-glare panel was black with the fin tip being grey. The 20" high fin code letter 'K' was yellow. The fuselage national marking was 30" diameter with the underwing national insignia being 18" diameter with the black underwing serials having a height of 16". The fin flash was 24" high and 18" wide with each colour segment being 6" wide.
References used: p274 *The Canadair Sabre*, by Larry Milbury, CANAV Books, 1986

Canadair Sabre F.4, XB918, 'R', of 130 Squadron, RAFG Bruggen, Germany, 1954.
Camouflage scheme of Dark Sea Grey and Dark Green over PRU Blue undersides.
XB918 has the earlier 130 Squadron markings consisting of a code letter in white superimposed on a 20" wide black disc applied to the fin. The anti-glare disc panel was black with the fin tip being grey. The fuselage national marking was 30" diameter with the underwing national insignia being 18" diameter with the black underwing serials having a height of 16". The fin flash was 24" high and 18" wide with each colour segment being 6" wide. References used: *Aircam No 20 Canadair & Commonwealth Sabre*, by Richard Ward, Aircam Aviation Series, 1971.

Canadair Sabre F.4, XB813, 'W', of 'C Flight', 229 OCU, RAF, Chivenor, 1954.
Camouflage scheme of Dark Sea Grey and Dark Green over PRU Blue undersides.
XB813 has the 229 OCU markings consisting of a 20" high code letter in white on the fin with the tip of the nose and wingtips painted red. The anti-glare panel was black with the fin tip being grey. The fuselage national marking was 30" diameter with the underwing national insignia being 18" diameter with the black underwing serials having a height of 16". The fin flash was 24" high and 18" wide with each colour segment being 6" wide.
References used: p99 *Wings of Fame Vol 10*, by Larry Davis, Aerospace Publishing, 1998.

Canadair Sabre F.4, XB872, 'W', of 'C Flight', 234 Squadron, RAFG, Geilenkirchen, 1955.
Camouflage scheme of Dark Sea Grey and Dark Green over PRU Blue undersides.
XB872 has the 234 Squadron markings consisting of a code letter in white and black fuselage bars with red diamonds superimposed within. Another 234 Squadron marking was the red nose edged in white and the black dragon within a white disc on the nose. The anti-glare panel was black with the fin tip being grey. The fuselage national marking was 30" diameter with the underwing national insignia being 18" diameter with the black underwing serials having a height of 16". The fin flash was 24" high and 18" wide with each colour segment being 6" wide.
References used: p266 *The Canadair Sabre*, by Larry Milbury, CANAV Books, 1986.

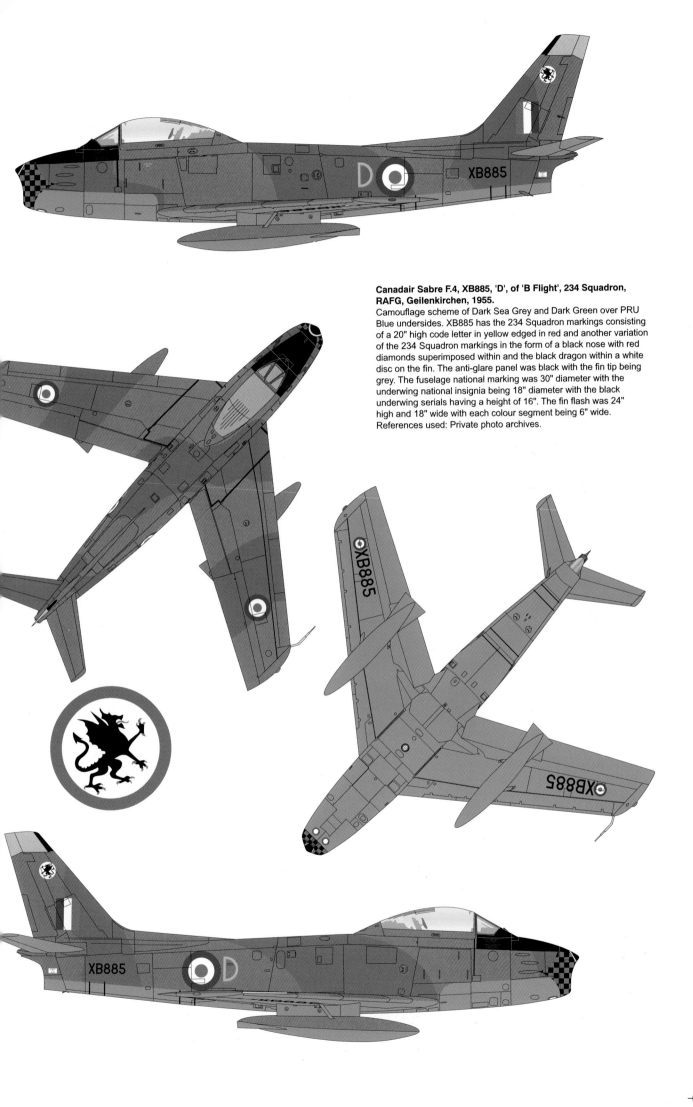

Canadair Sabre F.4, XB885, 'D', of 'B Flight', 234 Squadron, RAFG, Geilenkirchen, 1955.
Camouflage scheme of Dark Sea Grey and Dark Green over PRU Blue undersides. XB885 has the 234 Squadron markings consisting of a 20" high code letter in yellow edged in red and another variation of the 234 Squadron markings in the form of a black nose with red diamonds superimposed within and the black dragon within a white disc on the fin. The anti-glare panel was black with the fin tip being grey. The fuselage national marking was 30" diameter with the underwing national insignia being 18" diameter with the black underwing serials having a height of 16". The fin flash was 24" high and 18" wide with each colour segment being 6" wide.
References used: Private photo archives.

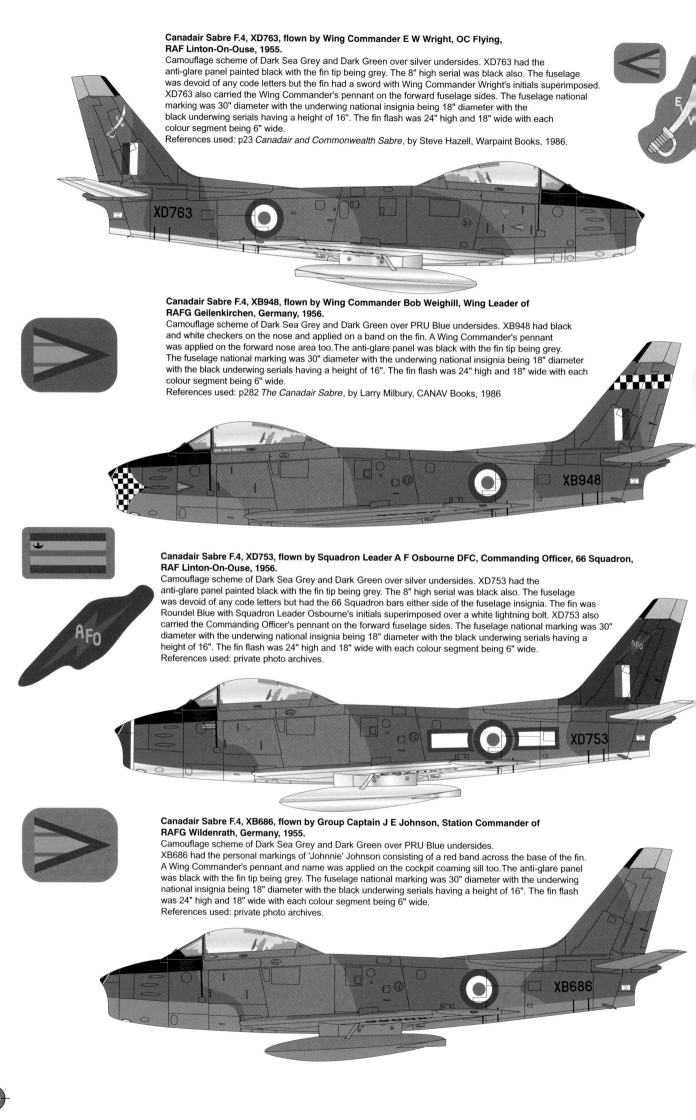

Canadair Sabre F.4, XD763, flown by Wing Commander E W Wright, OC Flying, RAF Linton-On-Ouse, 1955.
Camouflage scheme of Dark Sea Grey and Dark Green over silver undersides. XD763 had the anti-glare panel painted black with the fin tip being grey. The 8" high serial was black also. The fuselage was devoid of any code letters but the fin had a sword with Wing Commander Wright's initials superimposed. XD763 also carried the Wing Commander's pennant on the forward fuselage sides. The fuselage national marking was 30" diameter with the underwing national insignia being 18" diameter with the black underwing serials having a height of 16". The fin flash was 24" high and 18" wide with each colour segment being 6" wide.
References used: p23 *Canadair and Commonwealth Sabre*, by Steve Hazell, Warpaint Books, 1986.

Canadair Sabre F.4, XB948, flown by Wing Commander Bob Weighill, Wing Leader of RAFG Geilenkirchen, Germany, 1956.
Camouflage scheme of Dark Sea Grey and Dark Green over PRU Blue undersides. XB948 had black and white checkers on the nose and applied on a band on the fin. A Wing Commander's pennant was applied on the forward nose area too. The anti-glare panel was black with the fin tip being grey. The fuselage national marking was 30" diameter with the underwing national insignia being 18" diameter with the black underwing serials having a height of 16". The fin flash was 24" high and 18" wide with each colour segment being 6" wide.
References used: p282 *The Canadair Sabre*, by Larry Milbury, CANAV Books, 1986.

Canadair Sabre F.4, XD753, flown by Squadron Leader A F Osbourne DFC, Commanding Officer, 66 Squadron, RAF Linton-On-Ouse, 1956.
Camouflage scheme of Dark Sea Grey and Dark Green over silver undersides. XD753 had the anti-glare panel painted black with the fin tip being grey. The 8" high serial was black also. The fuselage was devoid of any code letters but had the 66 Squadron bars either side of the fuselage insignia. The fin was Roundel Blue with Squadron Leader Osbourne's initials superimposed over a white lightning bolt. XD753 also carried the Commanding Officer's pennant on the forward fuselage sides. The fuselage national marking was 30" diameter with the underwing national insignia being 18" diameter with the black underwing serials having a height of 16". The fin flash was 24" high and 18" wide with each colour segment being 6" wide.
References used: private photo archives.

Canadair Sabre F.4, XB686, flown by Group Captain J E Johnson, Station Commander of RAFG Wildenrath, Germany, 1955.
Camouflage scheme of Dark Sea Grey and Dark Green over PRU Blue undersides.
XB686 had the personal markings of 'Johnnie' Johnson consisting of a red band across the base of the fin. A Wing Commander's pennant and name was applied on the cockpit coaming sill too. The anti-glare panel was black with the fin tip being grey. The fuselage national marking was 30" diameter with the underwing national insignia being 18" diameter with the black underwing serials having a height of 16". The fin flash was 24" high and 18" wide with each colour segment being 6" wide.
References used: private photo archives.

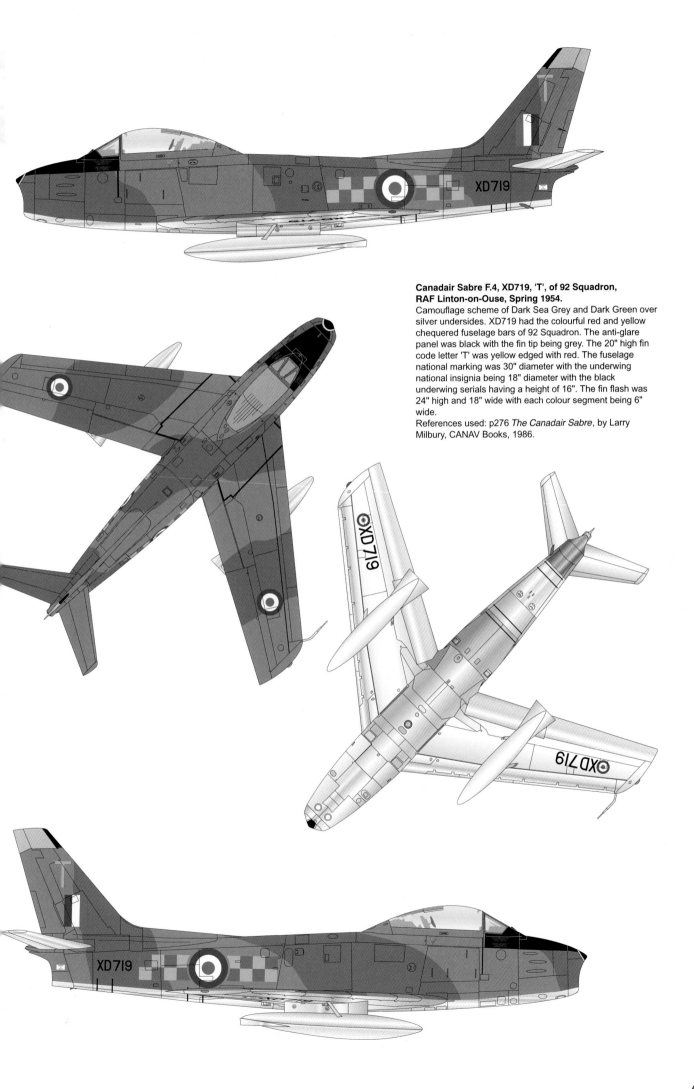

Canadair Sabre F.4, XD719, 'T', of 92 Squadron, RAF Linton-on-Ouse, Spring 1954.
Camouflage scheme of Dark Sea Grey and Dark Green over silver undersides. XD719 had the colourful red and yellow chequered fuselage bars of 92 Squadron. The anti-glare panel was black with the fin tip being grey. The 20" high fin code letter 'T' was yellow edged with red. The fuselage national marking was 30" diameter with the underwing national insignia being 18" diameter with the black underwing serials having a height of 16". The fin flash was 24" high and 18" wide with each colour segment being 6" wide.
References used: p276 *The Canadair Sabre*, by Larry Milbury, CANAV Books, 1986.

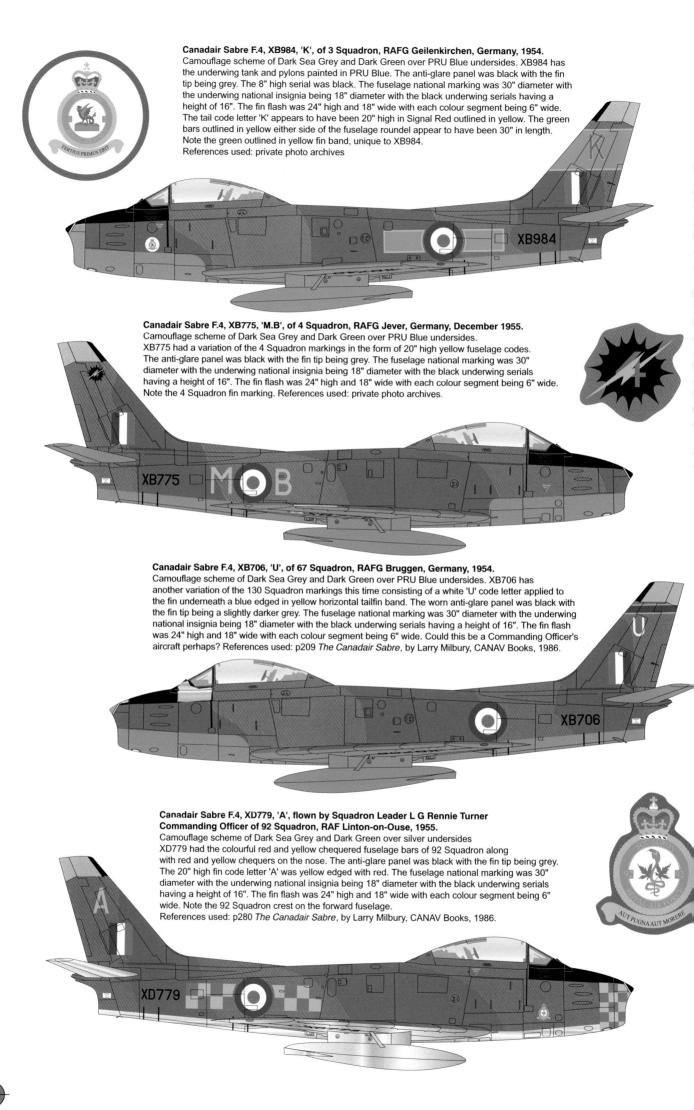

Canadair Sabre F.4, XB984, 'K', of 3 Squadron, RAFG Geilenkirchen, Germany, 1954.
Camouflage scheme of Dark Sea Grey and Dark Green over PRU Blue undersides. XB984 has the underwing tank and pylons painted in PRU Blue. The anti-glare panel was black with the fin tip being grey. The 8" high serial was black. The fuselage national marking was 30" diameter with the underwing national insignia being 18" diameter with the black underwing serials having a height of 16". The fin flash was 24" high and 18" wide with each colour segment being 6" wide. The tail code letter 'K' appears to have been 20" high in Signal Red outlined in yellow. The green bars outlined in yellow either side of the fuselage roundel appear to have been 30" in length. Note the green outlined in yellow fin band, unique to XB984.
References used: private photo archives

Canadair Sabre F.4, XB775, 'M.B', of 4 Squadron, RAFG Jever, Germany, December 1955.
Camouflage scheme of Dark Sea Grey and Dark Green over PRU Blue undersides.
XB775 had a variation of the 4 Squadron markings in the form of 20" high yellow fuselage codes. The anti-glare panel was black with the fin tip being grey. The fuselage national marking was 30" diameter with the underwing national insignia being 18" diameter with the black underwing serials having a height of 16". The fin flash was 24" high and 18" wide with each colour segment being 6" wide. Note the 4 Squadron fin marking. References used: private photo archives.

Canadair Sabre F.4, XB706, 'U', of 67 Squadron, RAFG Bruggen, Germany, 1954.
Camouflage scheme of Dark Sea Grey and Dark Green over PRU Blue undersides. XB706 has another variation of the 130 Squadron markings this time consisting of a white 'U' code letter applied to the fin underneath a blue edged in yellow horizontal tailfin band. The worn anti-glare panel was black with the fin tip being a slightly darker grey. The fuselage national marking was 30" diameter with the underwing national insignia being 18" diameter with the black underwing serials having a height of 16". The fin flash was 24" high and 18" wide with each colour segment being 6" wide. Could this be a Commanding Officer's aircraft perhaps? References used: p209 *The Canadair Sabre*, by Larry Milbury, CANAV Books, 1986.

Canadair Sabre F.4, XD779, 'A', flown by Squadron Leader L G Rennie Turner Commanding Officer of 92 Squadron, RAF Linton-on-Ouse, 1955.
Camouflage scheme of Dark Sea Grey and Dark Green over silver undersides
XD779 had the colourful red and yellow chequered fuselage bars of 92 Squadron along with red and yellow chequers on the nose. The anti-glare panel was black with the fin tip being grey. The 20" high fin code letter 'A' was yellow edged with red. The fuselage national marking was 30" diameter with the underwing national insignia being 18" diameter with the black underwing serials having a height of 16". The fin flash was 24" high and 18" wide with each colour segment being 6" wide. Note the 92 Squadron crest on the forward fuselage.
References used: p280 *The Canadair Sabre*, by Larry Milbury, CANAV Books, 1986.

Royal Canadian Air Force

By the late 1940s, the Royal Canadian Air Force was still operating piston-engined fighters, such as the North American F-51D and K Mustang. It was therefore a priority that a jet type be brought into service as soon as possible. There was a great feeling in Canada that a British jet fighter design should be purchased and that too much reliance was being placed on US products.

At this time, the only available British designs were the Gloster Meteor and the de Havilland Vampire. However, these designs were 'first generation jets', and new swept wing technology was now being utilised. The best fighter available at that time was the NA Sabre, and a deal was struck between the two countries that would enable the Sabre to be built under a licence agreement by Canadair Ltd.

Production begins

The first Canadair-built Sabre, was essentially identical to the F-86A and was built from sub-assemblies delivered by North American. This aircraft rolled off the production line in July 1950, and was designated Canadair CL-13 Sabre Mk 1. The first license-built F-86E, designated Canadair CL-13 Sabre Mk 2, was test flown in early 1951, and featured the US versions 'all flying' tailplane, a vast improvement over the original elevator type used on the F-86A/Sabre Mk 1. The aircraft also incorporated an optically flat windscreen.

The first Sabre Mk 2s entered service in April 1951, with No 410 'Cougar' Squadron, based at Dorval. Another two units, Nos 413 and 441 Squadrons were next, with more to follow.

RCAFSabre units began to be moved to Europe, under the overall command of No 1 Air Division. At this stage, the Cold War was starting to 'heat up', and Canada's Sabre contribution was a very welcome addition to the overall air defence of Western Europe.

The first Canadian squadrons to arrive were Nos 410 'Cougar', 439 'Sabre Tooth' and 441 'Silver Fox' Squadrons, making up No 1 Wing. These were based at RAF Luffenham in the UK, in November 1951. Nos 410 and 441 Squadrons were shipped over aboard the Canadian aircraft carrier *HMCS Magnificent*, whilst No 439 Sqn arrived via *'Leap Frog One'*. Essentially, this meant the aircraft flying in stages from Canada - Labrador - Greenland - Iceland - Scotland, and then on to Luffenham. Later the Wing transferred to Marville in France.

No 2 Wing came next, comprising Nos 416 'Black Lynx', 421 'Red Indian' and 430 'Silver Flacon' Squadrons, and was eventually stationed in France at Grostenquin. No 3 Wing arrived in early 1953, and comprised Nos 413 'Elephant', 427 'Lion', and 434 'Bluenose' Squadrons, based at Zweibrucken in Germany.

Finally, in September 1953, No 4 Wing arrived and was based at Baden-Soellingen. This unit comprised Nos 414 'Black Knight', 422 'Tomahawk' and 444 'Cobra' Squadrons and flew Sabre Mk 4s, although these were later passed on to the RAF.

The Sabre Mk.4 was the next major production variant, with various changes made, but it was still fitted with the US J47-GE-13 engine. Only a single Mk 3 had been manufactured, which was essentially a Mk 2, but fitted with the new Orenda 3 engine of Canadian design. The aircraft was built to exactly the same specification as the North American F-86J.

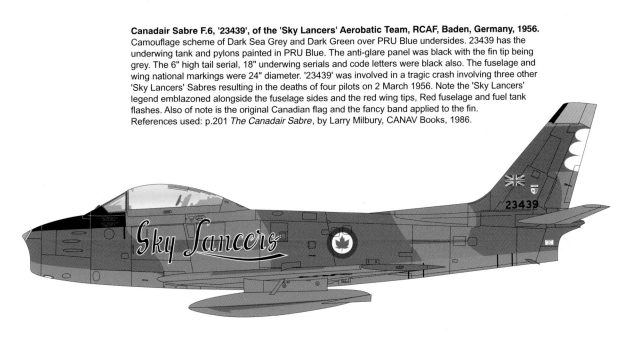

Canadair Sabre F.6, '23439', of the 'Sky Lancers' Aerobatic Team, RCAF, Baden, Germany, 1956.
Camouflage scheme of Dark Sea Grey and Dark Green over PRU Blue undersides. 23439 has the underwing tank and pylons painted in PRU Blue. The anti-glare panel was black with the fin tip being grey. The 6" high tail serial, 18" underwing serials and code letters were black also. The fuselage and wing national markings were 24" diameter. '23439' was involved in a tragic crash involving three other 'Sky Lancers' Sabres resulting in the deaths of four pilots on 2 March 1956. Note the 'Sky Lancers' legend emblazoned alongside the fuselage sides and the red wing tips, Red fuselage and fuel tank flashes. Also of note is the original Canadian flag and the fancy band applied to the fin.
References used: p.201 *The Canadair Sabre*, by Larry Milbury, CANAV Books, 1986.

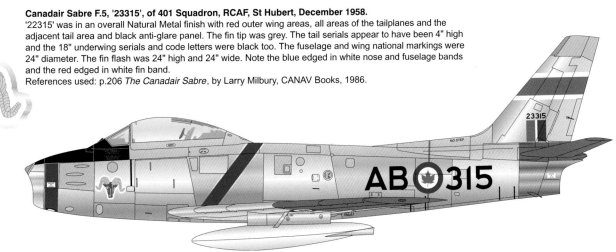

Canadair Sabre F.5, '23315', of 401 Squadron, RCAF, St Hubert, December 1958.
'22315' was in an overall Natural Metal finish with red outer wing areas, all areas of the tailplanes and the adjacent tail area and black anti-glare panel. The fin tip was grey. The tail serials appear to have been 4" high and the 18" underwing serials and code letters were black too. The fuselage and wing national markings were 24" diameter. The fin flash was 24" high and 24" wide. Note the blue edged in white nose and fuselage bands and the red edged in white fin band.
References used: p.206 *The Canadair Sabre*, by Larry Milbury, CANAV Books, 1986.

Canadair Sabre F.6, '23580', of 413 Squadron, RCAF, Prestwick, 1956.
Camouflage scheme of Dark Sea Grey and Dark Green over PRU Blue undersides. '23580' has the underwing tank and pylons painted in PRU Blue. The anti-glare panel was black with the fin tip being grey. The 6" high tail serial, 18" underwing serials and code letters were black also. The fuselage and wing national markings were 24" diameter. Note the 413 Squadron emblem superimposed on a Green horizontal tail band. Also of note is the original Canadian flag applied to the fin.
References used: p.181 *The Canadair Sabre*, by Larry Milbury, CANAV Books, 1986.

Canadair Sabre F.5, '23055', of 414 Squadron, RCAF, 1953.
Wearing a natural metal finish '23055' sports a non-standard style of code letters and numbers on the fuselage sides. The anti-glare panel was black with the fin tip being grey. The tail serial appears to have been 8" high with 18" high underwing serials and fuselage code letters which appear to have been 15" high were all black The fuselage and wing national markings were 30" diameter. Note the 414 Squadron emblem applied to the nose and the white and black striping on the fin and nose. Also of note is the original Canadian flag applied to the fin.
References used: p.200 *The Canadair Sabre*, by Larry Milbury, CANAV Books, 1986.

Canadair Sabre F.2, '19342', of 416 Squadron, RCAF, July 24, 1953.
Wearing a natural metal finish '19342' sports a non-standard style of code letter on the fuselage sides. The anti-glare panel was black with the fin tip being grey. The tail serial appears to have been 6" high with 18" high fuselage code letters which were all black The fuselage and wing national markings were 24" diameter. The fin flash was 15" wide and 20" high. Note the 416 Squadron emblem applied to the nose and the black and white diagonal fuselage striping on the forward fuselage. Also of note is the black rudder, nose and wing bands applied for 'Exercise Coronet'. Many thanks to Tom Calbury for his assistance with this profile.
References used: p.124 *The Canadair Sabre*, by Larry Milbury, CANAV Books, 1986.

Canadair Sabre F.2, '19350', of 421 Squadron, Sculthorpe, RCAF, 1950s.
'19350' sports the early natural metal finish. The anti-glare panel was black with the fin tip being grey. The tail serial appears to have been 6" high with 15" high fuselage code letters which were all black The fuselage and wing national markings were 24" diameter. Note the 421 Squadron emblem applied to the fin and the white and red striping on the fin and nose.
The fin flash was probably 18" wide and 20" high.
References used: p.126 *The Canadair Sabre*, by Larry Milbury, CANAV Books, 1986.

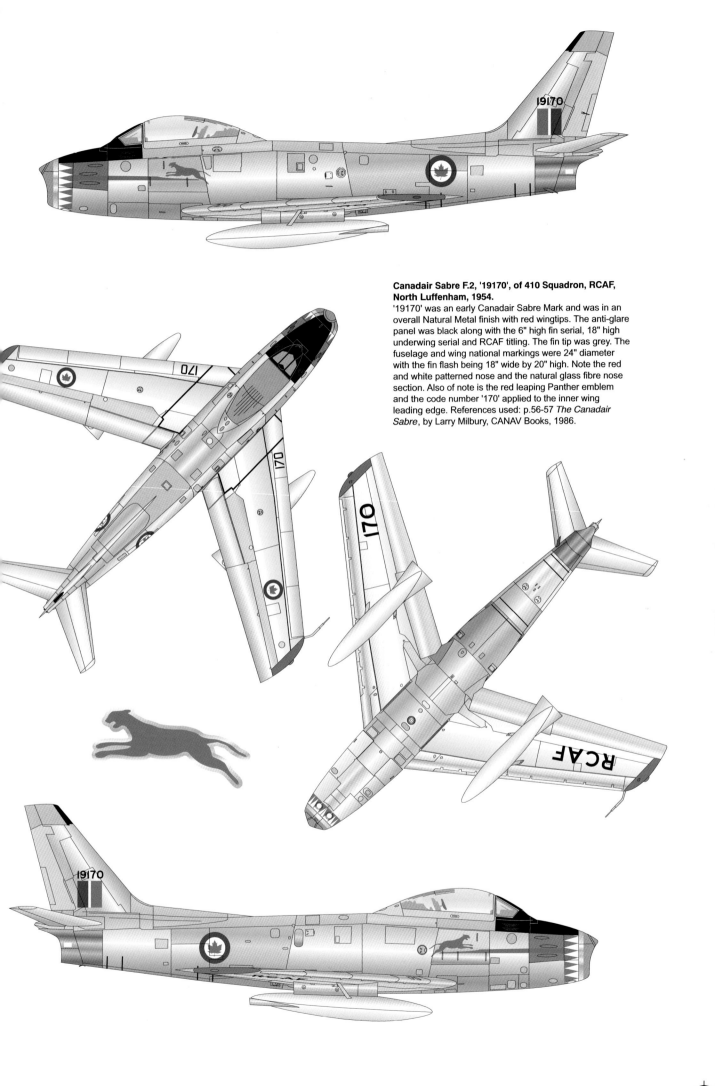

Canadair Sabre F.2, '19170', of 410 Squadron, RCAF, North Luffenham, 1954.

'19170' was an early Canadair Sabre Mark and was in an overall Natural Metal finish with red wingtips. The anti-glare panel was black along with the 6" high fin serial, 18" high underwing serial and RCAF titling. The fin tip was grey. The fuselage and wing national markings were 24" diameter with the fin flash being 18" wide by 20" high. Note the red and white patterned nose and the natural glass fibre nose section. Also of note is the red leaping Panther emblem and the code number '170' applied to the inner wing leading edge. References used: p.56-57 *The Canadair Sabre*, by Larry Milbury, CANAV Books, 1986.

Canadair Sabre F.2, '19355', of 430 Squadron, RCAF, Grostenquin, July, 1953.
Wearing a natural metal finish '19355' sports the anti-glare panel which was black along with the nose and wing bands, applied for 'Exercise Coronet' with the fin tip being grey. The tail serial appears to have been 6" high with 15" high fuselage code letters which again were black The fuselage and wing national markings were 24" diameter. Note the 430 Squadron emblem applied to the fin and the red lightning flash adorning the fuselage sides. The fin flash was 18" wide and 20" high. This F.2 carried the titling 'RCAF' in 18" high letters underneath the starboard wing.
References used: p.127 *The Canadair Sabre*, by Larry Milbury, CANAV Books, 1986.

Canadair Sabre F.2, '19102', of 431 Squadron, RCAF, Bagotville, January, 1954.
Wearing a natural metal finish '19102' was the first F.2 to be built and was assigned to the short lived 431 Squadron in January 1954. The anti-glare panel was black with the nose being natural fibre glass, the fin tip being grey. The tail serial appears to have been 6" high but no fuselage codes were applied to '19102' The fuselage and wing national markings were 24" diameter. Note the 431 'Iroquois' Squadron emblem applied to the nose. The fin flash was 18" wide and 20" high.
References used: p.48 *The Canadair Sabre*, by Larry Milbury, CANAV Books, 1986.

Canadair Sabre F.2, '19449', of 434 Squadron, RCAF, Istres, en-route to Rabat, 1950s.
'19449' is illustrated in the natural metal finish as seen on many early RCAF Sabres. The anti-glare panel was black with the nose being blue, the fin tip being grey. The tail serial appears to have been black and 6" high with 15" high black fuselage codes also. The fuselage and wing national markings were 24" in diameter. Note the 'Bluenose' schooner emblem superimposed on the blue fuselage chevron band.
References used: p.148 *The Canadair Sabre*, by Larry Milbury, CANAV Books, 1986.

Canadair Sabre F.5, '23110', of 438 Squadron, RCAF, St Hubert, March 1958.
'23110' is illustrated in the natural metal finish as seen on many early RCAF Sabres. The anti-glare panel was black with the nose tip and inner areas of the wing upper and lower surfaces being red, the fin tip being grey. The tail serial appears to have been black and 4" high with 15" high black fuselage codes also. The fuselage and wing national markings were 24" diameter. The fin flash was 18" wide by 20" high. Note the 438 Squadron emblem applied on the nose and the red outlined in white fuselage lightning flash.
References used: p.206 *The Canadair Sabre*, by Larry Milbury, CANAV Books, 1986.

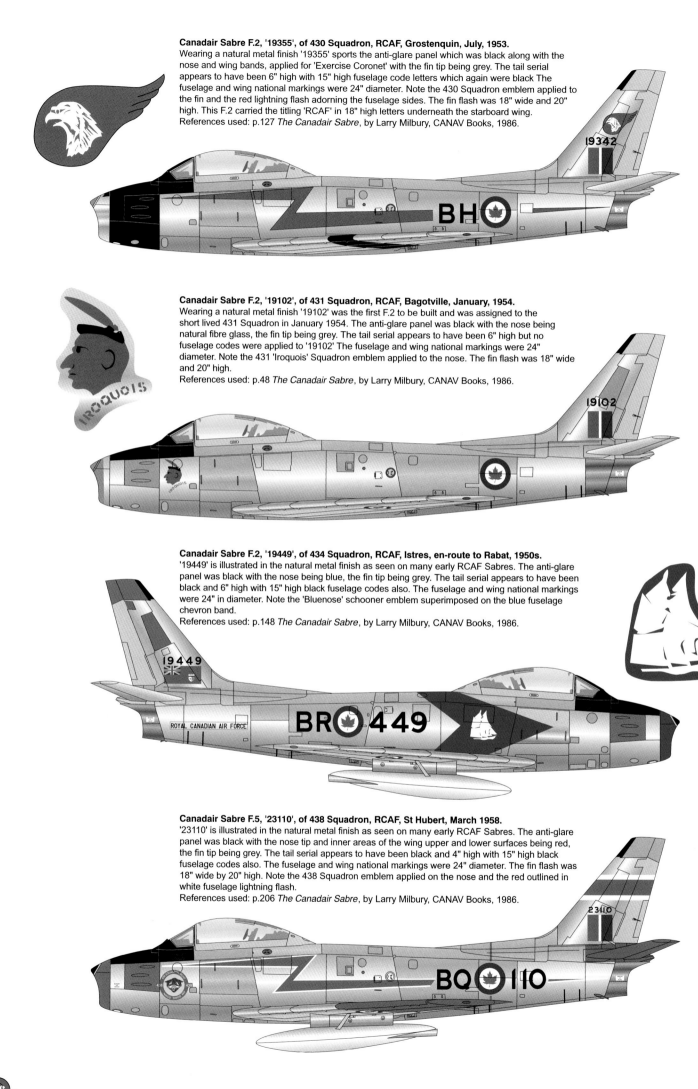

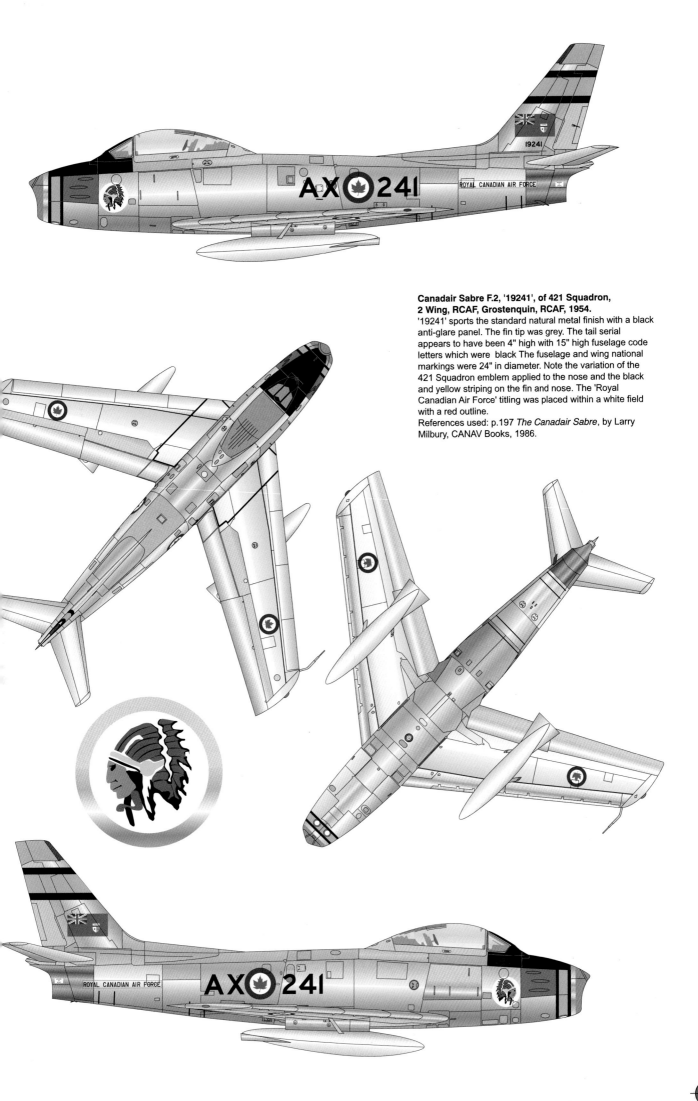

Canadair Sabre F.2, '19241', of 421 Squadron, 2 Wing, RCAF, Grostenquin, RCAF, 1954.
'19241' sports the standard natural metal finish with a black anti-glare panel. The fin tip was grey. The tail serial appears to have been 4" high with 15" high fuselage code letters which were black The fuselage and wing national markings were 24" in diameter. Note the variation of the 421 Squadron emblem applied to the nose and the black and yellow striping on the fin and nose. The 'Royal Canadian Air Force' titling was placed within a white field with a red outline.
References used: p.197 *The Canadair Sabre*, by Larry Milbury, CANAV Books, 1986.

Sabres Mk 5 and Mk 6

The Mk 5 was the first Sabre fitted with an engine of Canadian design and manufacture, the Orenda Mk 10. This engine had a slightly bigger diameter than the J47, and as on the Sabre Mk 3, the design had to be altered slightly internally to incorporate this change. The Mk 5 also introduced a fixed, wing leading edge, which replaced the extendable leading edge slats on previous variants. This improved the Mk 5s handling at high altitude, although it was found that the aircraft's low altitude manoeuvre characteristics were impaired somewhat.

However, the aircraft did show a marked improvement over the earlier Mk 2 and Mk 4, both in terms of speed, climb and range. In total some 370 Mk 5s were built, before being replaced by the final version, the Mk 6.

The Sabre Mk 6 was the ultimate Canadian-built Sabre, and was one of the best aircraft of its class. The automatic leading edge slats were re-introduced along with the wing extensions carried over from the Mk 5. This gave the aircraft excellent manoeuvreability at all speed ranges. The Orenda Mk 14 was used in this version, and gave improved thrust over the Mk 10.

Later in their career, Canadian-built Sabres were finished in Dark Green and Dark Sea Grey upper surfaces over PRU Blue undersides, like their RAF cousins, but still retained very colourful markings, steeped in squadron tradition.

The Sabre also lent itself very well to the aerobatic display role, with one of the more famous RCAF teams being the Golden Hawks, resplendent in an overall gold finish with red and white 'hawk' fuselage flashes.

The Sabre was finally withdrawn from RCAF service in 1968, long after it had been replaced by the F-104 Starfighter. Many airframes were passed on to other air forces, such as the West German *Luftwaffe*.

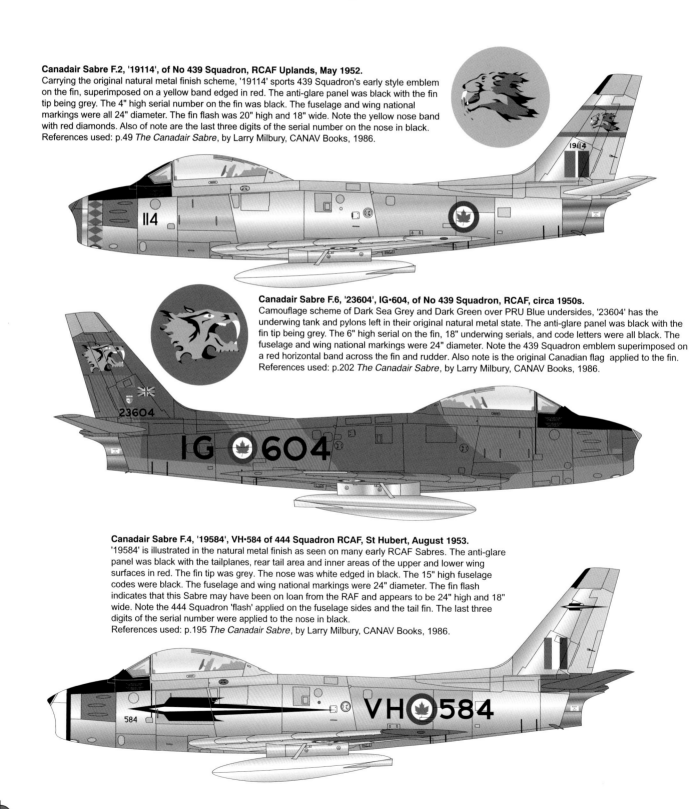

Canadair Sabre F.2, '19114', of No 439 Squadron, RCAF Uplands, May 1952.
Carrying the original natural metal finish scheme, '19114' sports 439 Squadron's early style emblem on the fin, superimposed on a yellow band edged in red. The anti-glare panel was black with the fin tip being grey. The 4" high serial number on the fin was black. The fuselage and wing national markings were all 24" diameter. The fin flash was 20" high and 18" wide. Note the yellow nose band with red diamonds. Also of note are the last three digits of the serial number on the nose in black.
References used: p.49 *The Canadair Sabre*, by Larry Milbury, CANAV Books, 1986.

Canadair Sabre F.6, '23604', IG·604, of No 439 Squadron, RCAF, circa 1950s.
Camouflage scheme of Dark Sea Grey and Dark Green over PRU Blue undersides, '23604' has the underwing tank and pylons left in their original natural metal state. The anti-glare panel was black with the fin tip being grey. The 6" high serial on the fin, 18" underwing serials, and code letters were all black. The fuselage and wing national markings were 24" diameter. Note the 439 Squadron emblem superimposed on a red horizontal band across the fin and rudder. Also note is the original Canadian flag applied to the fin.
References used: p.202 *The Canadair Sabre*, by Larry Milbury, CANAV Books, 1986.

Canadair Sabre F.4, '19584', VH·584 of 444 Squadron RCAF, St Hubert, August 1953.
'19584' is illustrated in the natural metal finish as seen on many early RCAF Sabres. The anti-glare panel was black with the tailplanes, rear tail area and inner areas of the upper and lower wing surfaces in red. The fin tip was grey. The nose was white edged in black. The 15" high fuselage codes were black. The fuselage and wing national markings were 24" diameter. The fin flash indicates that this Sabre may have been on loan from the RAF and appears to be 24" high and 18" wide. Note the 444 Squadron 'flash' applied on the fuselage sides and the tail fin. The last three digits of the serial number were applied to the nose in black.
References used: p.195 *The Canadair Sabre*, by Larry Milbury, CANAV Books, 1986.

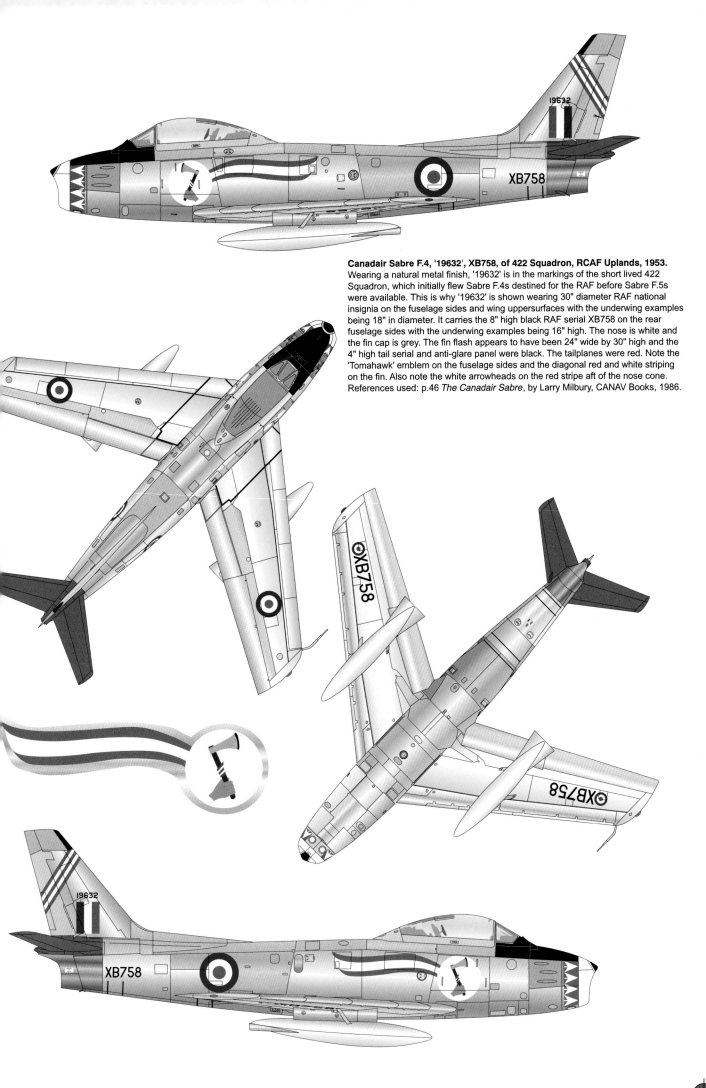

Canadair Sabre F.4, '19632', XB758, of 422 Squadron, RCAF Uplands, 1953.
Wearing a natural metal finish, '19632' is in the markings of the short lived 422 Squadron, which initially flew Sabre F.4s destined for the RAF before Sabre F.5s were available. This is why '19632' is shown wearing 30" diameter RAF national insignia on the fuselage sides and wing uppersurfaces with the underwing examples being 18" in diameter. It carries the 8" high black RAF serial XB758 on the rear fuselage sides with the underwing examples being 16" high. The nose is white and the fin cap is grey. The fin flash appears to have been 24" wide by 30" high and the 4" high tail serial and anti-glare panel were black. The tailplanes were red. Note the 'Tomahawk' emblem on the fuselage sides and the diagonal red and white striping on the fin. Also note the white arrowheads on the red stripe aft of the nose cone.
References used: p.46 *The Canadair Sabre*, by Larry Milbury, CANAV Books, 1986.

Above and Left: Canadiar Sabre Cl
Mk.4; BT-578-23578 of No 441 Squac
RCAF during the late 1950s. No 441 Squae
was based in Marville, France, during this t
The aircraft is weraing the final colour sch
of BS381C:638 Dark Sea Grey
BS381C:641 Dark Green upper surface can
flage with BS381C:636 PRU Blue undersi
RCAF roundels, in all six positions, and
original RCAF fin flash were carried with
441 Squadron's chequerboard fin markings

Photos: Adrian Balch

Below: Canadiar Sabre CL-13 Mk.6; IG•
23662, of No 439 Squadron, RCAF. Wea
the Dark Green/Dark Sea Grey/PRU Blue c
ouflage scheme and full colour Squadron
markings, it was photographed during a vis
RAF Waddington in 1959. No 439 Squae
was based at North Luffenham in England
ing this time.

Photo: Adrian Balch

CAC Sabre Mk 32, A94-
 No 76 Squadron's, 'Black
 r' Aerobatic Team, RAAF
 After the success of the
 Diamonds', a new team was
 d in the mid 1960s, featur-
 e Squadron badge of the
 g 'Black Panther'. These
 t carried the standard
 nium lacquer finish but had
 d red fin markings with the
 rs Head replaced by a
 d numeral '76'. They also
 a red diagonal flash over
 r fuselage and a a large
 Panther' below the cockpit
 er side.

*Private Collection - Rod
 har via Darren Mottram*

Left: CAC Sabre Mk 32, A94-930-30, of No 76 Squadron, 'Red Diamonds' Aerobatic Team, RAAF, based at Williamstown AFB in New South Wales in 1962. No 76 Squadron's famous aerobatic team used the Sabre for many years. All the team's aircraft carried the fuselage lightning bolt and Red Diamond with the Squadron number in white on either side of the fuselage. This particular aircraft also had the under wing fuel tanks painted with speciel markings and red tips. Standard Aluminium lacquer finish with black anti-glare panel. Red band around nose was outlined with a thin black stripe. Black serial and white nose codes. The front undercarriage door also had a white codes.

Photo: Private Collection - Rod Farquhar via Darren Mottram

Right: CAC Sabre Mk 32, A94-922, of No 76 Squadron, RAAF, circa 1961. This aircraft carried the standard RAAF finish of the period and the markings of No 76 Squadron. Aircraft Aluminium overall with black anti-glare panel, red nose band and wing tips with thin black stripes. Black tail codes, white nose and front undercarriage door codes. Light grey fin tip. Red fin markings with black stripes. White disk in fin markings with Black Panthers head. Fuselage roundels are standard RAAF 32 inch diameter with upper and under wing roundels in RAF style 42 inch diameter. Note the non standard fin flash.

Photo: Adrian Balch

Left: CAC Sabre Mk 31, A94-974-74 of No 3 Squadron, RAAF. This aircraft is now preserved in the RAAF Museum. Colour scheme is overall Aluminium lacquer with black anti-glare panel. Red nose intake band, outlined in white and red fin, emblazed with the Squadron marking comprising the Southern Cross in white. This aircraft still carried the standard RAF 42 inch diameter roundels on the upper and lower wing surfaces but carried the new RAAF 32 inch diameter roundels on either side of the fuselage. Compare this photograph with the artwork and rear cover top photograph. This photo shows the nose and front undercarriage codes in black.

Photo: Gary Madgwick/The Aviation Workshop Collection.

Left: CAC Sabre Mk 31, A94-901 of No 2 (F) OCU, 'Marksmen' Aerobatic Team, RAAF Williamstown, 1966.
A94-901 is wearing the yellow fin with black diagonal stripes, yellow nose cap and stylised 'Marksmen' lettering on either side of the fuselage below the cockpit. Standard overall Aluminium lacquer scheme with full 'Roo' roundels in all six positions. This scheme was one of the most attractive worn by 2 OCU. Of note are the lowered wing flaps, undercarriage doors, open speed brake and cockpit canopy.

Photo: Adrain Balch

Right: CAC Sabre Mk 32, A94-954 of No 2 (F) OCU, RAAF Williamstown, 1965, is wearing yet another version of the Squadron markings and colours comprising yellow and black fin markings. This time the complete fin was painted black and outlined in yellow. The aircraft still wears the RAF type roundels on the wings.

Photo: Private Collection - Rod Farquhar via Darren Mottram

Below: CAC Sabre Mk.31, A94-933 of No 2 (F) OTU/OCU, RAAF Williamstown, early 1960s, finished in one of the early schemes including the yellow and black fin markings complete with 'Tigers Head'. Nose cap is yellow with black stripe. Serial and codes are also black.

Photo: Errol OHara via Darren Mottram

Bottom left: CAC Sabre Mk 32, A94-945 of No 5 (F) OCU, RAAF Williamstown, mid-1960s. Standard Aluminium lacquer scheme, this aircraft is sporting full Australian Roo markings on the wings and carried Black nose codes. It is also seen carrying 167 gallon ferry tanks.
Photo: Greg Meggs

Below right: CAC Sabre Mk 32, A94-949 of No 2 (F) OCU, RAAF Williamstown, 1969. Note the special fin markings of the Squadron's 'Leaping Tiger' over a yellow band. Full details of this aircraft can be seen on p35. Overall Aluminium colour scheme with yellow nose cap. By the late 1960s, all RAAF aircraft carried Australian 'Roo roundels in all six positions.
Photo: Dick Hails via Darren Mottram

Canadair Sabre F.6, '23560', of 444 Squadron RCAF, Baden, Germany, 1950s.
Camouflage scheme of Dark Sea Grey and Dark Green over PRU Blue undersides with the underwing tank and pylons also painted in PRU Blue. The anti-glare panel was black with the fin tip in grey. The 6" high tail serial, 18" fuselage and wing code letters were also black. The fuselage and wing national markings were 24" in diameter. Note the later rendition of the 444 Squadron emblem superimposed on a white edged in black fin band.
References used: p.160 *The Canadair Sabre*, by Larry Milbury, CANAV Books, 1986.

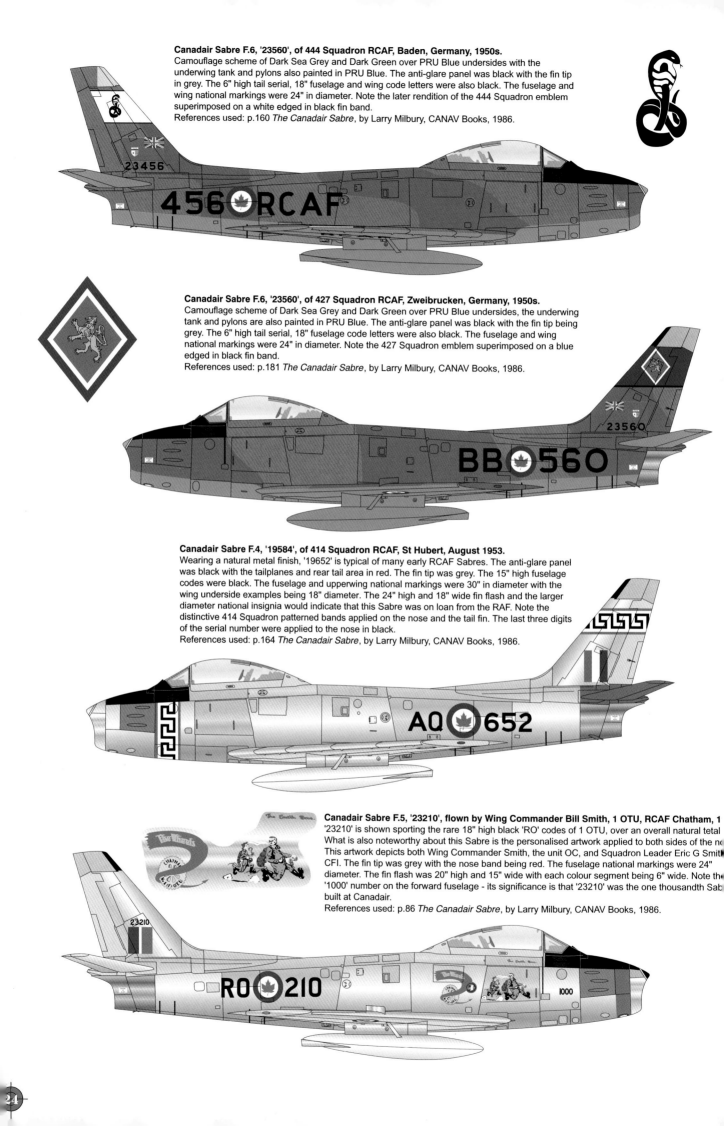

Canadair Sabre F.6, '23560', of 427 Squadron RCAF, Zweibrucken, Germany, 1950s.
Camouflage scheme of Dark Sea Grey and Dark Green over PRU Blue undersides, the underwing tank and pylons are also painted in PRU Blue. The anti-glare panel was black with the fin tip being grey. The 6" high tail serial, 18" fuselage code letters were also black. The fuselage and wing national markings were 24" in diameter. Note the 427 Squadron emblem superimposed on a blue edged in black fin band.
References used: p.181 *The Canadair Sabre*, by Larry Milbury, CANAV Books, 1986.

Canadair Sabre F.4, '19584', of 414 Squadron RCAF, St Hubert, August 1953.
Wearing a natural metal finish, '19652' is typical of many early RCAF Sabres. The anti-glare panel was black with the tailplanes and rear tail area in red. The fin tip was grey. The 15" high fuselage codes were black. The fuselage and upperwing national markings were 30" in diameter with the wing underside examples being 18" diameter. The 24" high and 18" wide fin flash and the larger diameter national insignia would indicate that this Sabre was on loan from the RAF. Note the distinctive 414 Squadron patterned bands applied on the nose and the tail fin. The last three digits of the serial number were applied to the nose in black.
References used: p.164 *The Canadair Sabre*, by Larry Milbury, CANAV Books, 1986.

Canadair Sabre F.5, '23210', flown by Wing Commander Bill Smith, 1 OTU, RCAF Chatham, 1
'23210' is shown sporting the rare 18" high black 'RO' codes of 1 OTU, over an overall natural tetal
What is also noteworthy about this Sabre is the personalised artwork applied to both sides of the n
This artwork depicts both Wing Commander Smith, the unit OC, and Squadron Leader Eric G Smith
CFI. The fin tip was grey with the nose band being red. The fuselage national markings were 24"
diameter. The fin flash was 20" high and 15" wide with each colour segment being 6" wide. Note the
'1000' number on the forward fuselage - its significance is that '23210' was the one thousandth Sab
built at Canadair.
References used: p.86 *The Canadair Sabre*, by Larry Milbury, CANAV Books, 1986.

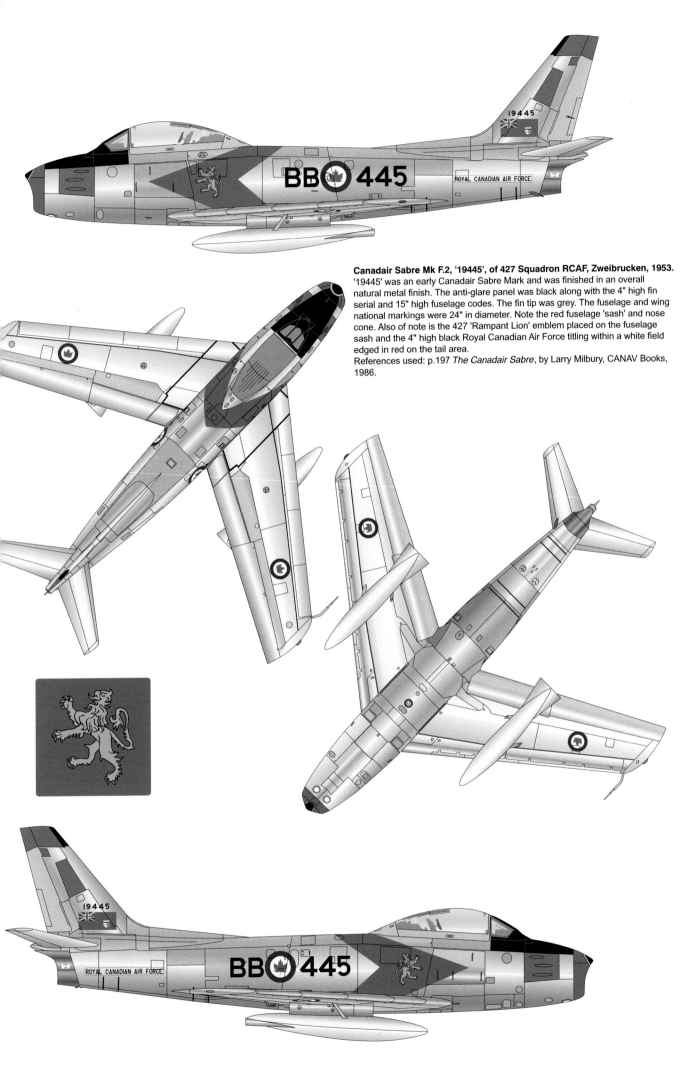

Canadair Sabre Mk F.2, '19445', of 427 Squadron RCAF, Zweibrucken, 1953.
'19445' was an early Canadair Sabre Mark and was finished in an overall natural metal finish. The anti-glare panel was black along with the 4" high fin serial and 15" high fuselage codes. The fin tip was grey. The fuselage and wing national markings were 24" in diameter. Note the red fuselage 'sash' and nose cone. Also of note is the 427 'Rampant Lion' emblem placed on the fuselage sash and the 4" high black Royal Canadian Air Force titling within a white field edged in red on the tail area.
References used: p.197 *The Canadair Sabre*, by Larry Milbury, CANAV Books, 1986.

ROYAL CANADIAN AIR FORCE

BB 445

19445

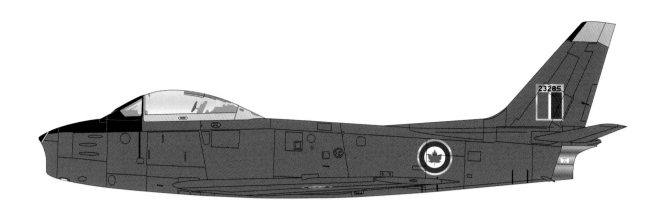

Canadair Sabre F.5, '23285', 1955 Toronto Air Show, Trenton, September 1955.
'23285' was given this overall red paint scheme for the Toronto Air Show in 1955. The anti-glare panel was black with the fin tip being grey. The national markings were 24" in diameter throughout with a 'halo' of the natural metal finish around the outer edges. The fin flash was 20" high and 18" wide with each colour segment being 6" wide. The tail serial was 4" high. References used: p.199 *The Canadair Sabre*, by Larry Milbury, CANAV Books, 1986.

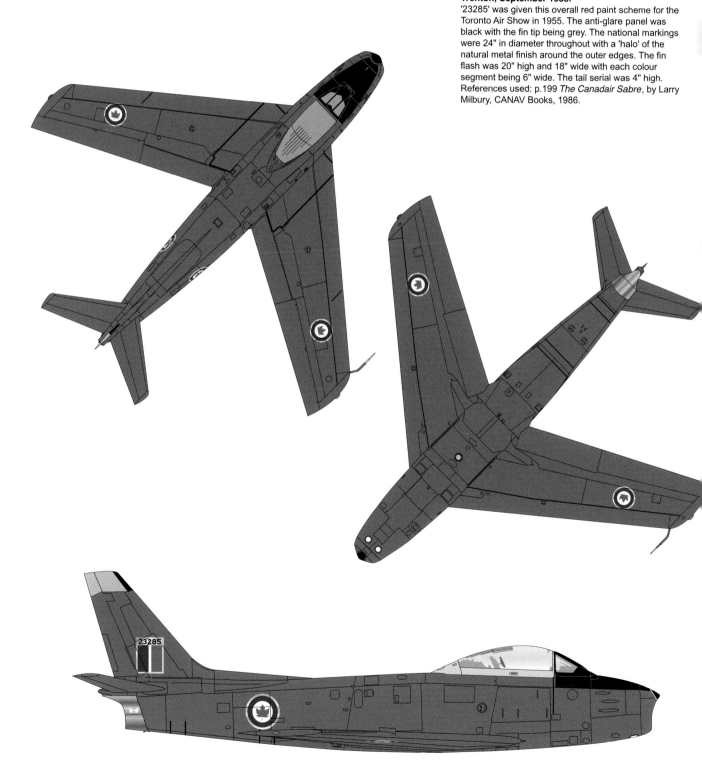

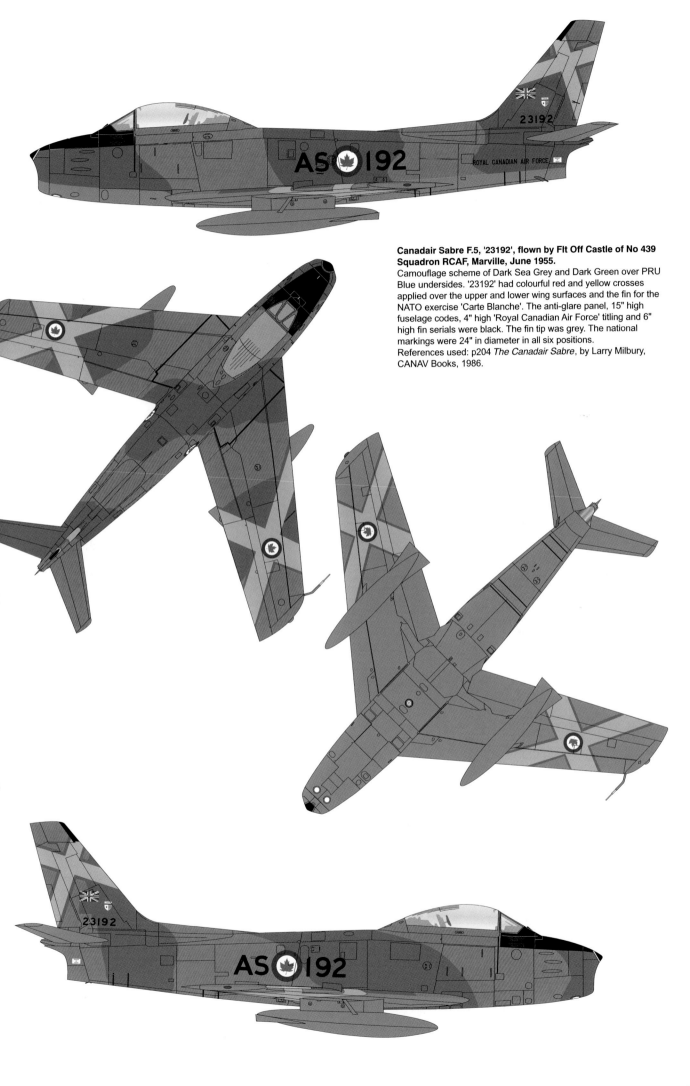

Canadair Sabre F.5, '23192', flown by Flt Off Castle of No 439 Squadron RCAF, Marville, June 1955.

Camouflage scheme of Dark Sea Grey and Dark Green over PRU Blue undersides. '23192' had colourful red and yellow crosses applied over the upper and lower wing surfaces and the fin for the NATO exercise 'Carte Blanche'. The anti-glare panel, 15" high fuselage codes, 4" high 'Royal Canadian Air Force' titling and 6" high fin serials were black. The fin tip was grey. The national markings were 24" in diameter in all six positions.

References used: p204 *The Canadair Sabre*, by Larry Milbury, CANAV Books, 1986.

Royal Australian Air Force

As with their British and Canadian counterparts, the advent of the MiG-15 prompted a drive to procure a modern jet design for RAAF service. It was becoming apparent that the Gloster Meteor and de Havilland Vampire just could not 'cut it' in air-to-air combat against the nimble Russian fighter, as the Australians found out in the Korean War, with the Meteor F 8. As was the case with Canada, the only suitable type then available was the Sabre.

As good as the Sabre was, the RAAF was looking for more speed and more destructive firepower. As the J-47 engine of the current F-86F model did not deliver the amount of thrust to get the required speed, a change of engine was necessary.

With this in mind, the RAAF opted for the British Rolls-Royce RA-7 Avon. There was little size difference between this engine and the J-47, but the Avon delivered 7,500lbs of thrust compared to the J-47's 5,910lbs. There was a penalty however. The Avon weighed some 181kg, (400lbs), less than the J-47. This would have an adverse effect in the aircraft's centre of gravity, so a major redesign would be required to incorporate the Avon into the F-86 design.

The first aspect of this was the re-location of the engine further aft to re-balance the aircraft. The fuselage break points were also moved aft as the engine mounts had to be relocated. The forward section of the fuselage was lengthened slightly by incorporating a plug, whilst the aft section was shortened to balance this. These changes had the effect of deepening the fuselage, although the length remained the same as for other Sabres. The nose intake was also increased in diameter to take into account the increased airflow needed for the new engine. The jet nozzle and exhaust empennage was increased in size to allow for the extra thrust that was generated.

The problem of increasing the aircraft's firepower was also addressed. The six 12.7mm, (0.5 inch), Colt-Browning machine guns were replaced by two 30mm Aden cannon, with one either side of the nose, in the original machine gun positions. The port gun was mounted some 20mm further aft of the starboard one, whilst the latter was mounted in an inverted position. Later in its career, the Commonwealth Aircraft Corporation (CAC) CA-27 Sabre Mk 32, as it would be designated, was also equipped with a pair of the new Philco-Ford AIM-9B Sidewinder air-to-air missiles, carried on launch shoe pylons mounted slightly inboard of the main gear.

The prototype CAC Sabre, designated CA-26 first flew in August 1953 from Avalon RAAF base. This initial flight was promising, and an order was placed by the RAAF for 111 examples. The first twenty-two aircraft of this batch, designated CA-27 Mk 30s were fitted with slatted wings and Avon RA-7 engines, and were essentially very similar to the prototype. The next twenty aircraft, designated Mk 31s, were fitted with Avon 20 engines, (the RA-7 now being built under license), and non-slatted wings but with extended leading edges. The remaining aircraft from this batch were designated Mk 32s and were fitted with the Avon 26, and as previously mentioned, wing hard points to take Sidewinder AAMs, bombs, drop tanks or rockets.

Between August 1953 and December 1961, the Commonwealth Aircraft Corporation built a total of 112 Sabres.

RAAF Sabres saw service during the Vietnam War, flying air patrols over US bases within Thailand and the type led a long career, spanning some 25 years in RAAF service.

By 1971, all had been withdrawn. Ex-Australian machines were passed on to other air forces in the region. In 1969, the Royal Malaysian Air Force took delivery of eighteen Mk 32s, with Indonesia acquiring eighteen aircraft of the same type in 1973. Malaysia passed on some of its ex-service Sabres to this air force in 1976.

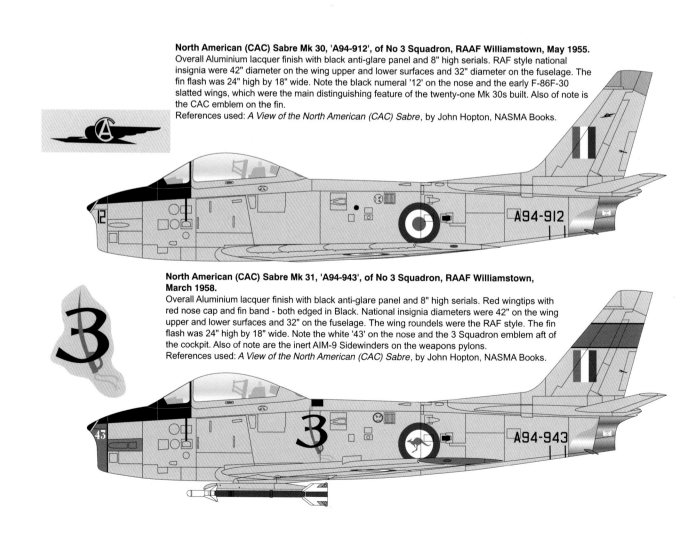

North American (CAC) Sabre Mk 30, 'A94-912', of No 3 Squadron, RAAF Williamstown, May 1955.
Overall Aluminium lacquer finish with black anti-glare panel and 8" high serials. RAF style national insignia were 42" diameter on the wing upper and lower surfaces and 32" diameter on the fuselage. The fin flash was 24" high by 18" wide. Note the black numeral '12' on the nose and the early F-86F-30 slatted wings, which were the main distinguishing feature of the twenty-one Mk 30s built. Also of note is the CAC emblem on the fin.
References used: *A View of the North American (CAC) Sabre*, by John Hopton, NASMA Books.

North American (CAC) Sabre Mk 31, 'A94-943', of No 3 Squadron, RAAF Williamstown, March 1958.
Overall Aluminium lacquer finish with black anti-glare panel and 8" high serials. Red wingtips with red nose cap and fin band - both edged in Black. National insignia diameters were 42" on the wing upper and lower surfaces and 32" on the fuselage. The wing roundels were the RAF style. The fin flash was 24" high by 18" wide. Note the white '43' on the nose and the 3 Squadron emblem aft of the cockpit. Also of note are the inert AIM-9 Sidewinders on the weapons pylons.
References used: *A View of the North American (CAC) Sabre*, by John Hopton, NASMA Books.

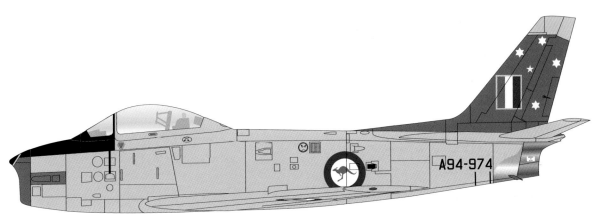

North American (CAC) Sabre Mk 31, 'A94-974', of No 3 Squadron, RAAF Butterworth, Malaysia, May 1958.
No 3 Squadron changed their markings to this style in early 1958. Overall Aluminium lacquer finish with black anti-glare panel and 8" high serials. Red fin emblazoned with a white 'Southern Cross' emblem and a red nose cap. The RAF style national insignia diameters were 42" on the wing upper and lower surfaces and the RAAF style insignia were 32" diameter on the fuselage. The fin flash was 24" high by 18" wide. Note the 'halo' where the original silver finish has been left around the fin flash. Note also the 'No Step' marking stripes on the outer areas of the wing upper surfaces.
References used: private photo archives of Rod Farquhar via Darren Mottram (Aus).

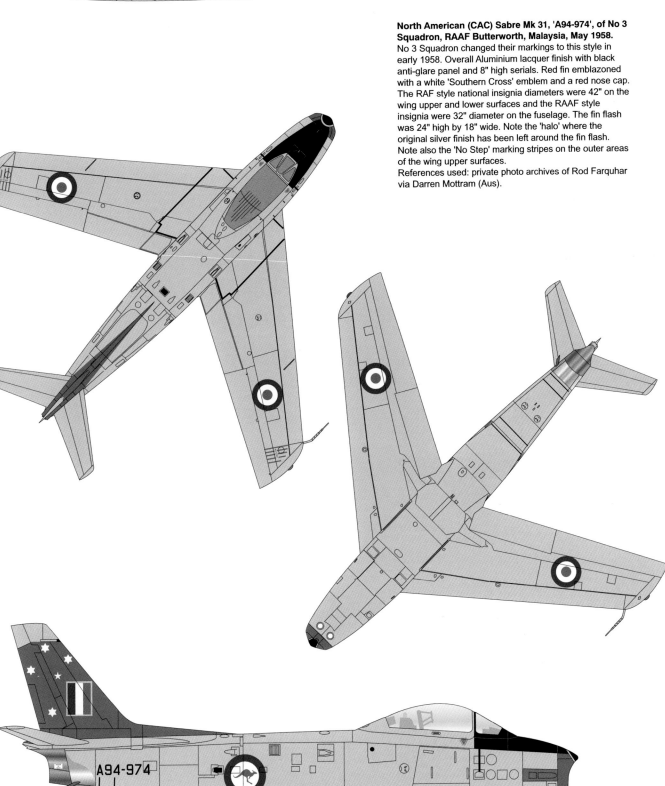

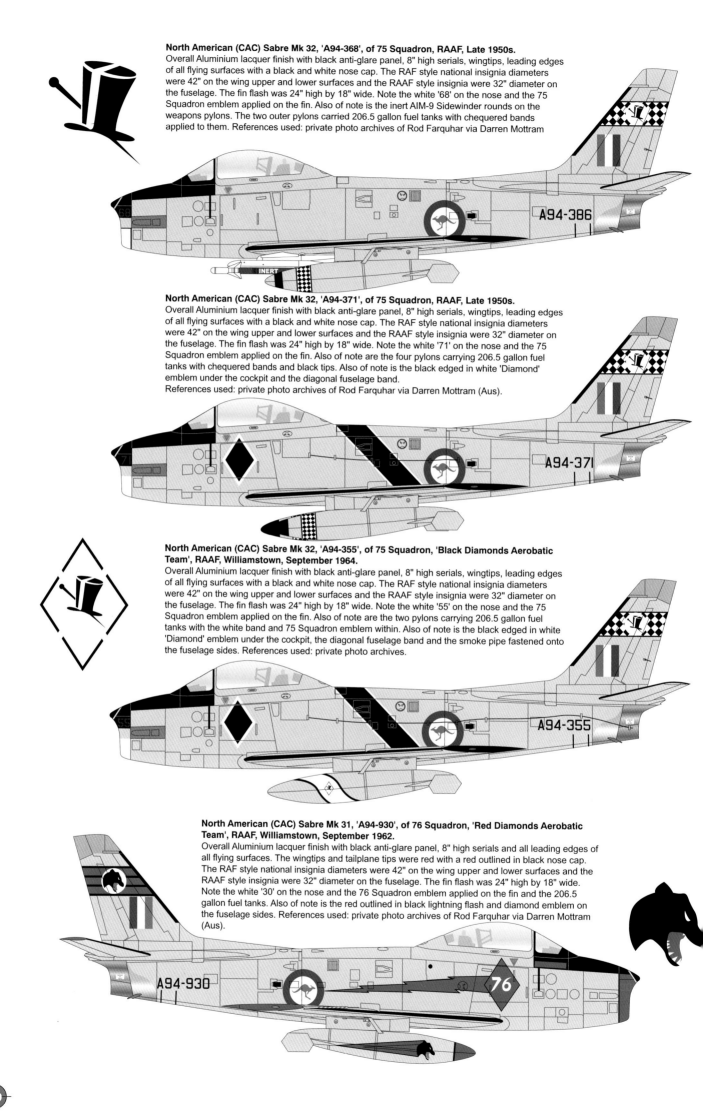

North American (CAC) Sabre Mk 32, 'A94-368', of 75 Squadron, RAAF, Late 1950s.
Overall Aluminium lacquer finish with black anti-glare panel, 8" high serials, wingtips, leading edges of all flying surfaces with a black and white nose cap. The RAF style national insignia diameters were 42" on the wing upper and lower surfaces and the RAAF style insignia were 32" diameter on the fuselage. The fin flash was 24" high by 18" wide. Note the white '68' on the nose and the 75 Squadron emblem applied on the fin. Also of note is the inert AIM-9 Sidewinder rounds on the weapons pylons. The two outer pylons carried 206.5 gallon fuel tanks with chequered bands applied to them. References used: private photo archives of Rod Farquhar via Darren Mottram

North American (CAC) Sabre Mk 32, 'A94-371', of 75 Squadron, RAAF, Late 1950s.
Overall Aluminium lacquer finish with black anti-glare panel, 8" high serials, wingtips, leading edges of all flying surfaces with a black and white nose cap. The RAF style national insignia diameters were 42" on the wing upper and lower surfaces and the RAAF style insignia were 32" diameter on the fuselage. The fin flash was 24" high by 18" wide. Note the white '71' on the nose and the 75 Squadron emblem applied on the fin. Also of note are the four pylons carrying 206.5 gallon fuel tanks with chequered bands and black tips. Also of note is the black edged in white 'Diamond' emblem under the cockpit and the diagonal fuselage band.
References used: private photo archives of Rod Farquhar via Darren Mottram (Aus).

North American (CAC) Sabre Mk 32, 'A94-355', of 75 Squadron, 'Black Diamonds Aerobatic Team', RAAF, Williamstown, September 1964.
Overall Aluminium lacquer finish with black anti-glare panel, 8" high serials, wingtips, leading edges of all flying surfaces with a black and white nose cap. The RAF style national insignia diameters were 42" on the wing upper and lower surfaces and the RAAF style insignia were 32" diameter on the fuselage. The fin flash was 24" high by 18" wide. Note the white '55' on the nose and the 75 Squadron emblem applied on the fin. Also of note are the two pylons carrying 206.5 gallon fuel tanks with the white band and 75 Squadron emblem within. Also of note is the black edged in white 'Diamond' emblem under the cockpit, the diagonal fuselage band and the smoke pipe fastened onto the fuselage sides. References used: private photo archives.

North American (CAC) Sabre Mk 31, 'A94-930', of 76 Squadron, 'Red Diamonds Aerobatic Team', RAAF, Williamstown, September 1962.
Overall Aluminium lacquer finish with black anti-glare panel, 8" high serials and all leading edges of all flying surfaces. The wingtips and tailplane tips were red with a red outlined in black nose cap. The RAF style national insignia diameters were 42" on the wing upper and lower surfaces and the RAAF style insignia were 32" diameter on the fuselage. The fin flash was 24" high by 18" wide. Note the white '30' on the nose and the 76 Squadron emblem applied on the fin and the 206.5 gallon fuel tanks. Also of note is the red outlined in black lightning flash and diamond emblem on the fuselage sides. References used: private photo archives of Rod Farquhar via Darren Mottram (Aus).

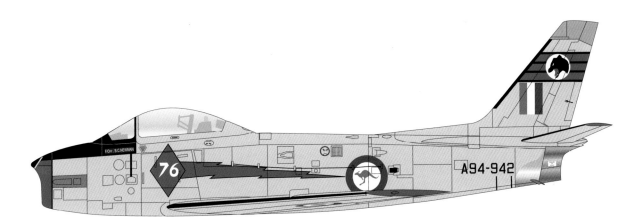

North American (CAC) Sabre Mk 32, 'A94-942', of 76 Squadron, 'Red Diamonds Aerobatic Team', RAAF, Williamstown, September 1962.
Overall Aluminium lacquer finish with black anti-glare panel, 8" high serials and all leading edges of all flying surfaces. The wingtips and tailplane tips were red with a red outlined in black nose cap. RAF style national insignia diameters were 42" on the wing upper and lower surfaces and the RAAF style national insignia were 32" diameter on the fuselage. The fin flash was 24" high by 18" wide. Note the white '30' on the nose and the 76 Squadron emblem applied on the fin. Also of note is the red outlined in black lightning flash and diamond emblem on the fuselage sides.
References used: private photo archives.

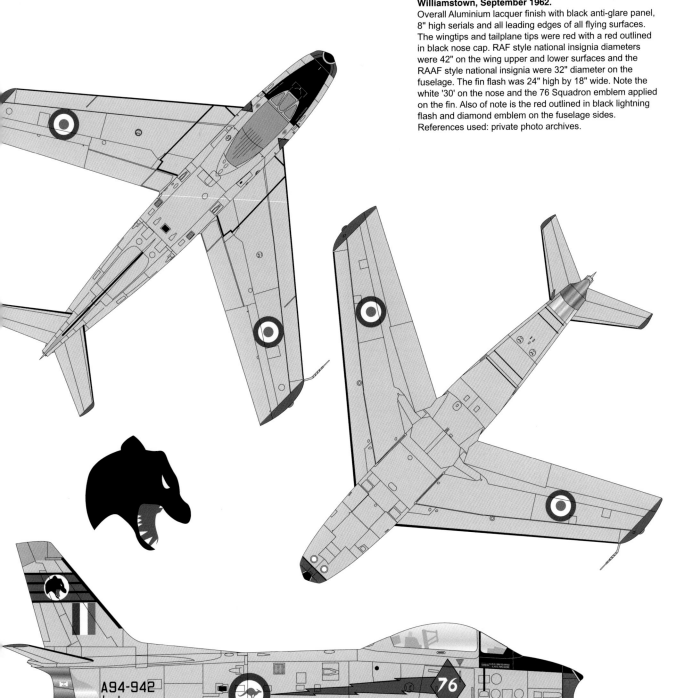

North American (CAC) Sabre Mk 32, 'A94-368', of 76 Squadron, 'Black Panther Aerobatic Team', RAAF Williamstown, February 1965.

Overall Aluminium lacquer finish with black anti-glare panel, 8" high serials and all leading edges of all flying surfaces. The wingtips and tailplane tips were red with a red outlined in black nose cap.The RAF style national insignia diameters were 42" on the wing upper and lower surfaces and the RAAF style insignia were 32" diameter on the fuselage.The fin flash was 24" high by 18" wide. Note the white '68' on the nose and the 76 Squadron emblem applied on the fin and the 'Black Panther' emblem below the cockpit. Also of note is the red outlined in black diagonal flash on the fuselage sides. References used: private photo archives of Rod Farquhar via Darren Mottram (Aus).

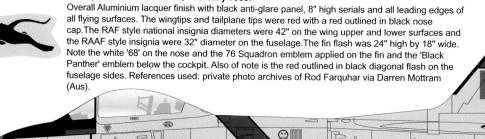

North American (CAC) Sabre Mk 32, 'A94-965', of 77 Squadron, RAAF Butterworth, Malaya, 1963.

Overall Aluminium lacquer finish with black anti-glare panel and 8" high serials. The RAF style national insignia diameters were 42" on the wing upper and lower surfaces and the RAAF style insignia were 32" diameter on the fuselage.The fin flash was 24" high by 18" wide. Note the green edged with black nose and the green and white chequered tailfin band edged in black. References used: private photo archives.

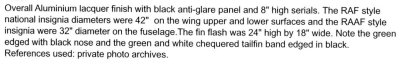

North American (CAC) Sabre Mk 32, 'A94-974), of 77 Squadron, RAAF Butterworth, Malaya, late 1960s.

'A94-974' has an overall Aluminium lacquer finish with black anti-glare panel with 8" high serials. The wingtips and tailplane tips were green edged with black along with the nose cap. A post-1966 Sabre wearing the RAAF styled national insignia with diameters of 42" on the wing upper and lower surfaces and 32" on the fuselage.The fin flash was 24" high by 18" wide. Note the green and white chequered tailfin band edged in black, and the eight underwing rockets. References used: private photo archives of Rod Farquhar via Darren Mottram (Aus).

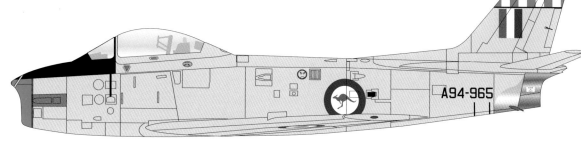

North American (CAC) Sabre Mk 32, 'A94-965', of 77 Squadron, RAAF Butterworth, Malaya, 1968.

Shown five years later, 'A94-965' still has an overall Aluminium lacquer finish with black anti-glare panel with 8" high serials. The wingtips and tailplane tips were green edged with black along with the nose cap. By 1966, the RAAF style national insignia was carried on the CAC Sabres with diameters of 42" on the wing upper and lower surfaces and 32" diameter on the fuselage.The fin flash was 24" high by 18" wide. Note the green and white chequered tailfin band edged in black and the small fuel tank emblem. References used: private photo archives.

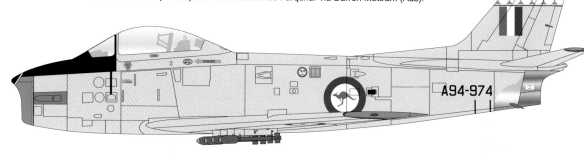

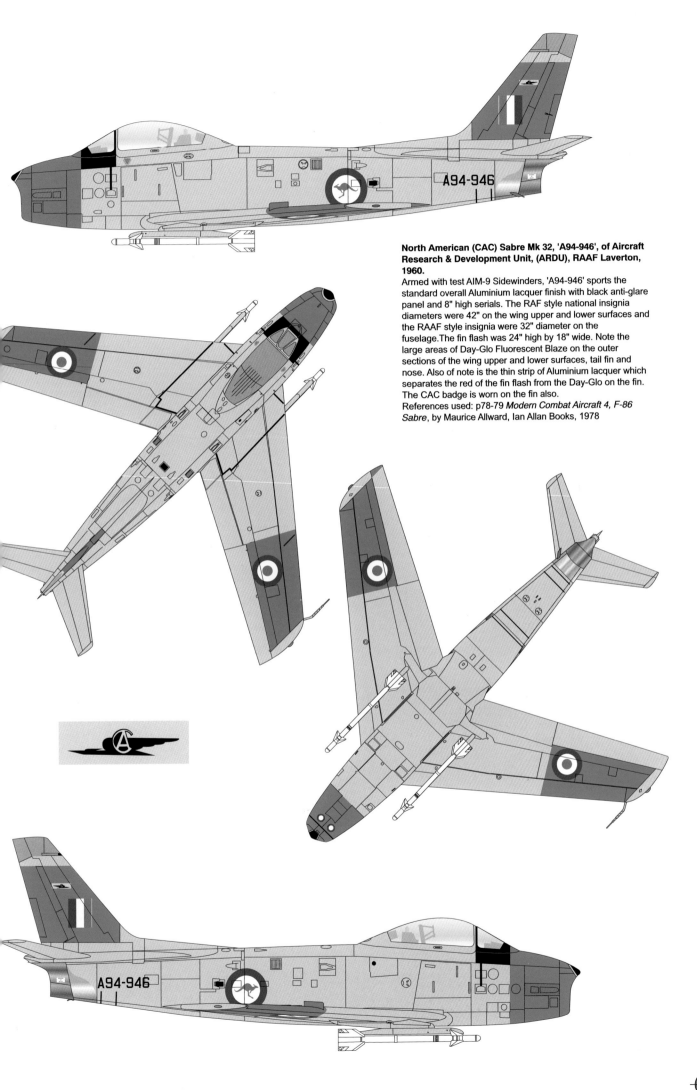

North American (CAC) Sabre Mk 32, 'A94-946', of Aircraft Research & Development Unit, (ARDU), RAAF Laverton, 1960.

Armed with test AIM-9 Sidewinders, 'A94-946' sports the standard overall Aluminium lacquer finish with black anti-glare panel and 8" high serials. The RAF style national insignia diameters were 42" on the wing upper and lower surfaces and the RAAF style insignia were 32" diameter on the fuselage.The fin flash was 24" high by 18" wide. Note the large areas of Day-Glo Fluorescent Blaze on the outer sections of the wing upper and lower surfaces, tail fin and nose. Also of note is the thin strip of Aluminium lacquer which separates the red of the fin flash from the Day-Glo on the fin. The CAC badge is worn on the fin also.

References used: p78-79 *Modern Combat Aircraft 4, F-86 Sabre*, by Maurice Allward, Ian Allan Books, 1978

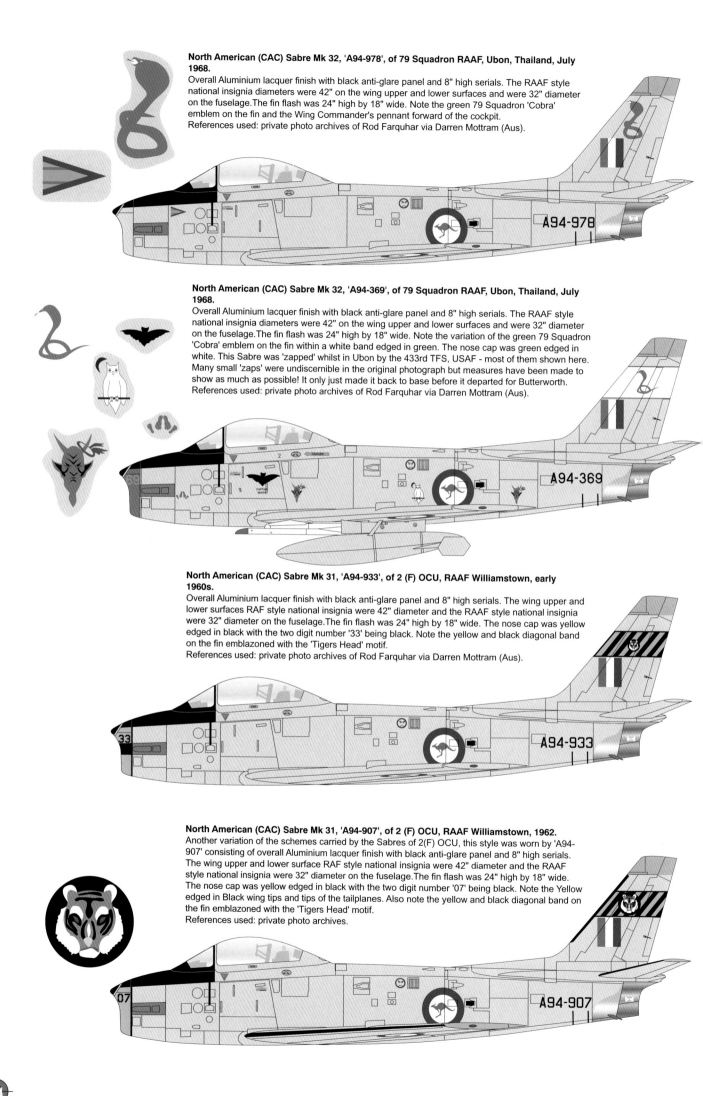

North American (CAC) Sabre Mk 32, 'A94-978', of 79 Squadron RAAF, Ubon, Thailand, July 1968.
Overall Aluminium lacquer finish with black anti-glare panel and 8" high serials. The RAAF style national insignia diameters were 42" on the wing upper and lower surfaces and were 32" diameter on the fuselage.The fin flash was 24" high by 18" wide. Note the green 79 Squadron 'Cobra' emblem on the fin and the Wing Commander's pennant forward of the cockpit.
References used: private photo archives of Rod Farquhar via Darren Mottram (Aus).

North American (CAC) Sabre Mk 32, 'A94-369', of 79 Squadron RAAF, Ubon, Thailand, July 1968.
Overall Aluminium lacquer finish with black anti-glare panel and 8" high serials. The RAAF style national insignia diameters were 42" on the wing upper and lower surfaces and were 32" diameter on the fuselage.The fin flash was 24" high by 18" wide. Note the variation of the green 79 Squadron 'Cobra' emblem on the fin within a white band edged in green. The nose cap was green edged in white. This Sabre was 'zapped' whilst in Ubon by the 433rd TFS, USAF - most of them shown here. Many small 'zaps' were undiscernible in the original photograph but measures have been made to show as much as possible! It only just made it back to base before it departed for Butterworth.
References used: private photo archives of Rod Farquhar via Darren Mottram (Aus).

North American (CAC) Sabre Mk 31, 'A94-933', of 2 (F) OCU, RAAF Williamstown, early 1960s.
Overall Aluminium lacquer finish with black anti-glare panel and 8" high serials. The wing upper and lower surfaces RAF style national insignia were 42" diameter and the RAAF style national insignia were 32" diameter on the fuselage.The fin flash was 24" high by 18" wide. The nose cap was yellow edged in black with the two digit number '33' being black. Note the yellow and black diagonal band on the fin emblazoned with the 'Tigers Head' motif.
References used: private photo archives of Rod Farquhar via Darren Mottram (Aus).

North American (CAC) Sabre Mk 31, 'A94-907', of 2 (F) OCU, RAAF Williamstown, 1962.
Another variation of the schemes carried by the Sabres of 2(F) OCU, this style was worn by 'A94-907' consisting of overall Aluminium lacquer finish with black anti-glare panel and 8" high serials. The wing upper and lower surface RAF style national insignia were 42" diameter and the RAAF style national insignia were 32" diameter on the fuselage.The fin flash was 24" high by 18" wide. The nose cap was yellow edged in black with the two digit number '07' being black. Note the Yellow edged in Black wing tips and tips of the tailplanes. Also note the yellow and black diagonal band on the fin emblazoned with the 'Tigers Head' motif.
References used: private photo archives.

North American (CAC) Sabre Mk 32, 'A94-949', of 2 (F) OCU, RAAF, Williamstown, late 1960s.
This scheme carried by 'A94-949' comprised an overall Aluminium lacquer finish with black anti-glare panel and 8" high serials. The wing upper and lower surface RAAF style national insignia were 42" diameter with the fuselage national insignia being 32" diameter.The angled fin flash was 24" high by 18" wide. The nose cap was yellow edged in black. Note the black leading edges to the wings and tailplanes. Also note the non-standard 'Leaping Tiger' superimposed on the yellow fin band. This Sabre carried the 206.5 gallon fuel tanks.
References used: private photo archives of Rod Farquhar via Darren Mottram (Aus).

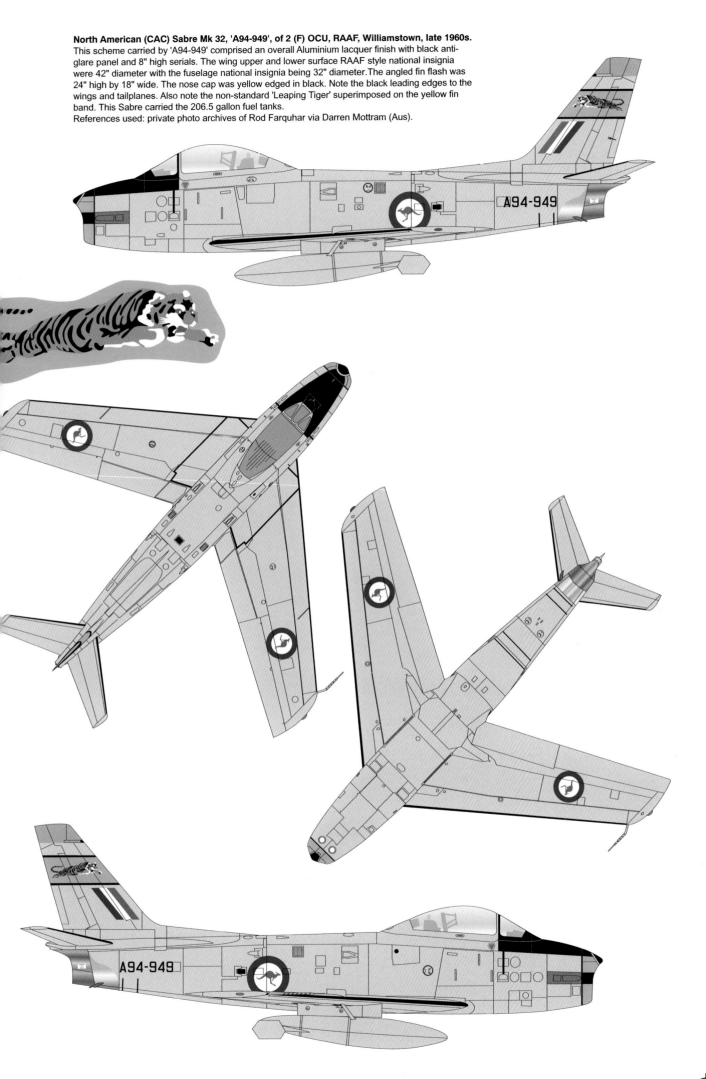

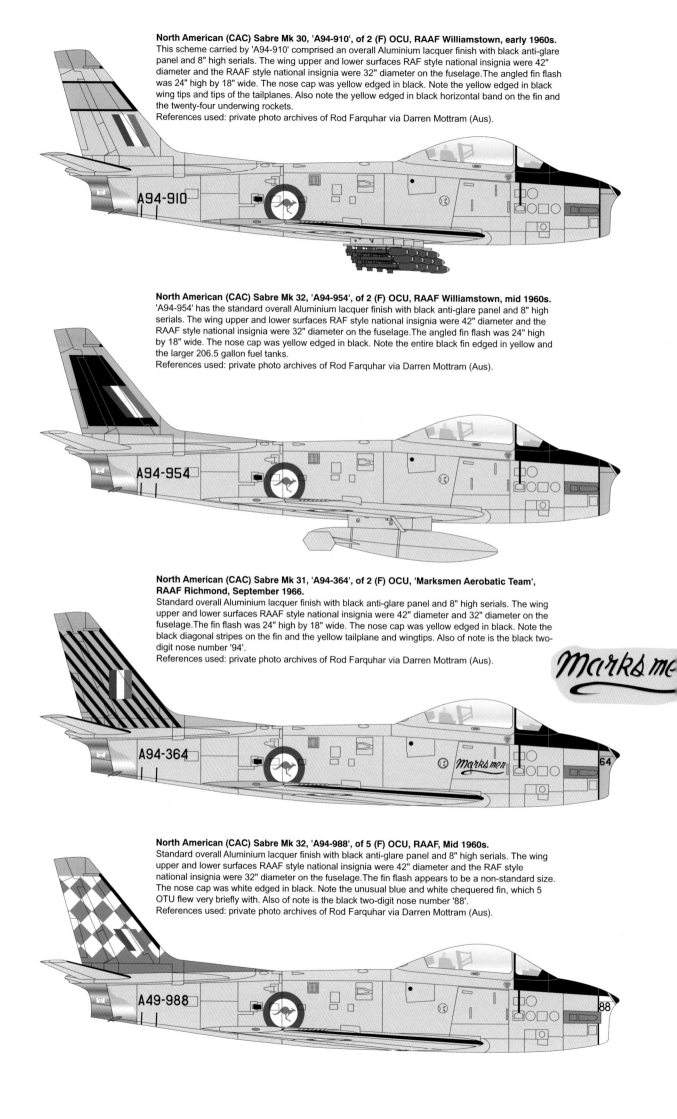

North American (CAC) Sabre Mk 30, 'A94-910', of 2 (F) OCU, RAAF Williamstown, early 1960s.
This scheme carried by 'A94-910' comprised an overall Aluminium lacquer finish with black anti-glare panel and 8" high serials. The wing upper and lower surfaces RAF style national insignia were 42" diameter and the RAAF style national insignia were 32" diameter on the fuselage. The yellow edged in black wing fin flash was 24" high by 18" wide. The nose cap was yellow edged in black. Note the yellow edged in black wing tips and tips of the tailplanes. Also note the yellow edged in black horizontal band on the fin and the twenty-four underwing rockets.
References used: private photo archives of Rod Farquhar via Darren Mottram (Aus).

North American (CAC) Sabre Mk 32, 'A94-954', of 2 (F) OCU, RAAF Williamstown, mid 1960s.
'A94-954' has the standard overall Aluminium lacquer finish with black anti-glare panel and 8" high serials. The wing upper and lower surfaces RAF style national insignia were 42" diameter and the RAAF style national insignia were 32" diameter on the fuselage. The angled fin flash was 24" high by 18" wide. The nose cap was yellow edged in black. Note the entire black fin edged in yellow and the larger 206.5 gallon fuel tanks.
References used: private photo archives of Rod Farquhar via Darren Mottram (Aus).

North American (CAC) Sabre Mk 31, 'A94-364', of 2 (F) OCU, 'Marksmen Aerobatic Team', RAAF Richmond, September 1966.
Standard overall Aluminium lacquer finish with black anti-glare panel and 8" high serials. The wing upper and lower surfaces RAAF style national insignia were 42" diameter and 32" diameter on the fuselage. The fin flash was 24" high by 18" wide. The nose cap was yellow edged in black. Note the black diagonal stripes on the fin and the yellow tailplane and wingtips. Also of note is the black two-digit nose number '94'.
References used: private photo archives of Rod Farquhar via Darren Mottram (Aus).

North American (CAC) Sabre Mk 32, 'A94-988', of 5 (F) OCU, RAAF, Mid 1960s.
Standard overall Aluminium lacquer finish with black anti-glare panel and 8" high serials. The wing upper and lower surfaces RAAF style national insignia were 42" diameter and the RAF style national insignia were 32" diameter on the fuselage. The fin flash appears to be a non-standard size. The nose cap was white edged in black. Note the unusual blue and white chequered fin, which 5 OTU flew very briefly with. Also of note is the black two-digit nose number '88'.
References used: private photo archives of Rod Farquhar via Darren Mottram (Aus).

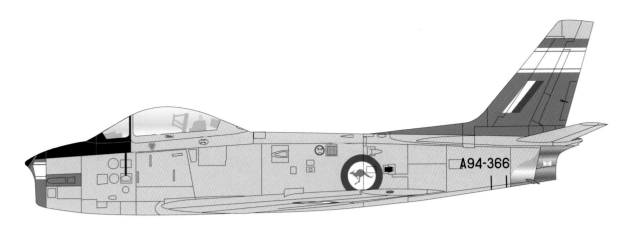

North American (CAC) Sabre Mk 32, 'A94-366', of 5 (F) OCU, RAAF, Mid 1960s.
Standard overall Aluminium lacquer finish with black anti-glare panel and 8" high serials. The wing upper and lower surfaces RAAF style national insignia were 42" diameter and the RAF style national insignia were 32" diameter on the fuselage. The angled fin flash appears to be 24" high and 18" wide. The nose cap was blue with white bands. Note the later blue fin with white bands. Also of note are the 'No Step' markings on the wing tips.
References used: private photo archives of Rod Farquhar via Darren Mottram (Aus).

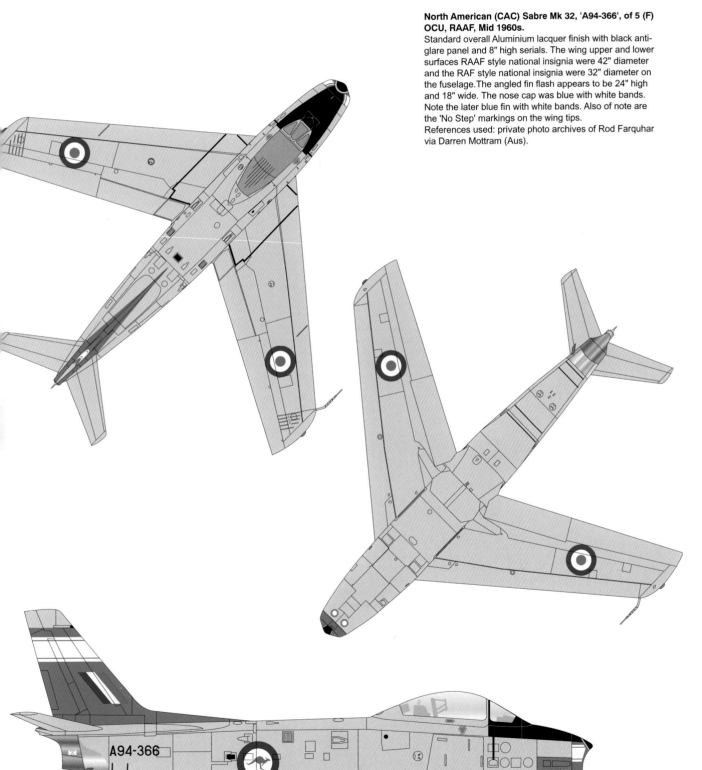

South African Air Force

The other principal and major Commonwealth user of the Sabre was South Africa, who operated the type during the Korean War. No 2 Squadron, SAAF, newly equipped with the Sabre after operating F-51D Mustangs, flew twenty-two F-86Fs on loan from the United States, under the command of the US 18th Fighter Bomber Wing, based at K-55, (Osan).

The SAAF aircraft showed a lot of commonality of markings with their US allies, apart from the adoption of South African 'Springbok' roundels and large fin flash stripes. The 18th FBW's two US units, (the 12th and 67th Fighter Bomber Squadrons), also adopted the practice of applying these large fin stripes to the fins of their F-86s.

Although their operational service on the Sabre in this Theatre was short, during the Korean War, No 2 Squadron flew over 2000 missions, the majority of which were fighter/bomber strikes, gaining an impressive reputation.

On leaving the Korean peninsula at the end of the war, No 2 Squadron returned its Sabres back over to the USAF, who subsequently passed many of these aircraft to the Nationalist Chinese Air Force in Taiwan.

In 1954, the SAAF bought thirty-four Canadair Sabre Mk 6s, and these were operated by Nos 1 and 2 Squadrons, based at Pietersberg and Waterkloof respectively.

In 1961, the 'Springbok' type roundel was discarded for the five point castelated device, which was actually a stylized representation of the Cape Town Fort. The fin flash tri-colour was retained however, along with the natural metal finish.

By the 1970s, SAAF Sabres were being re-finished in an attractive Olive Drab and Tan upper surface disruptive camouflage scheme over Light Grey undersurfaces.

By this time though, the Sabre was long overdue for replacement in SAAF service, with the Dassault Mirage III taking over its role fully by 1979.

During the wind-down, some aircraft were passed on to No 85 AFS, (Advanced Flying School), in 1980. Some ex-SAAF Sabres were sold to private collectors following complete withdrawal from SAAF service.

North American Sabre F-86F-30, '611', 'F', 'DANNY BOY', flown by Lt John Koekemoer, of No 2 Squadron, SAAF, K55 Osan AB, Korea, 1953.
'611' was in an overall Natural Metal finish with the Far Eastern Air Force Theatre marking around the mid-fuselage and wing tips consisting of a 28" wide yellow band edged with 4" wide black edges. The fin tip was grey. The serials on the rear fuslage were 15" high in black with the aircraft letter 'F' being 42" high. The national insignia were 30" diameter on the wing upper and lower surfaces with the fuselage examples being 36" diameter. The 'DANNY BOY' titling was 8" high in black. The fin flash was 84" high and 27" wide. Note the 2 Squadron emblem on the nose.
References used: p.27 *South African Colours and Markings Vol 1 No.4*, by Piet Van Schalkwyk, William Marshall and Stefaan Bouwer, Colour and Markings Books, 2002.

North American Sabre F-86F-30, '606', 'L', 'TOMTIT', of No 2 Squadron, SAAF, K55 Osan AB, Korea, 1953.
'606' was also in an overall Natural Metal finish with the Far Eastern Air Force Theatre marking around the mid-fuselage and wing tips consisting of a 28" wide yellow band with 4" wide black edges. The fin tip was grey. The rear fuselage serials were 15" high in black with the aircraft letter 'L' 42" high. The national insignia were 30" diameter on the wing upper and lower surfaces with the fuselage examples being 36" diameter. The 'TOMTIT' titling was 8" high in black. The fin flash was 84" high and 27" wide. Note the 2 Squadron emblem on the nose.
References used: p.26 *South African Colours and Markings Vol 1 No.4*, by Piet Van Schalkwyk, William Marshall and Stefaan Bouwer, Colour and Markings Books, 2002.

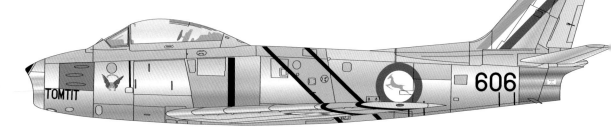

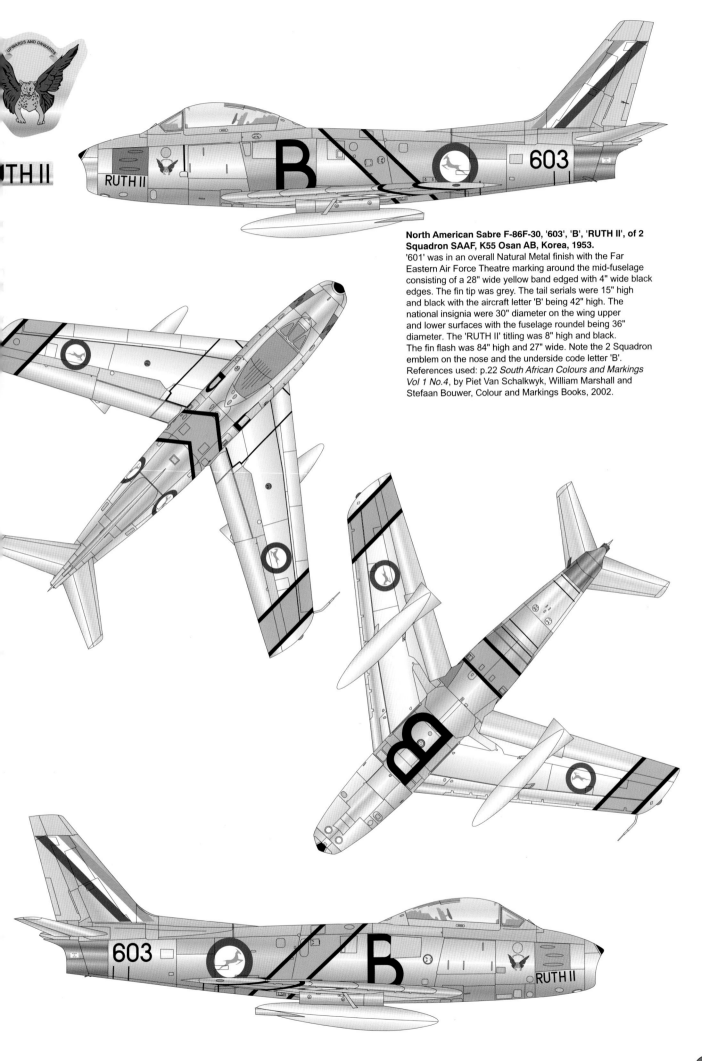

North American Sabre F-86F-30, '603', 'B', 'RUTH II', of 2 Squadron SAAF, K55 Osan AB, Korea, 1953.

'601' was in an overall Natural Metal finish with the Far Eastern Air Force Theatre marking around the mid-fuselage consisting of a 28" wide yellow band edged with 4" wide black edges. The fin tip was grey. The tail serials were 15" high and black with the aircraft letter 'B' being 42" high. The national insignia were 30" diameter on the wing upper and lower surfaces with the fuselage roundel being 36" diameter. The 'RUTH II' titling was 8" high and black. The fin flash was 84" high and 27" wide. Note the 2 Squadron emblem on the nose and the underside code letter 'B'.
References used: p.22 *South African Colours and Markings Vol 1 No.4*, by Piet Van Schalkwyk, William Marshall and Stefaan Bouwer, Colour and Markings Books, 2002.

North American Sabre F-86F-30, '616', 'Q', of 2 Squadron SAAF, K55 Osan AB, Korea, 1953.
'616' was in an overall Natural Metal finish with the Far Eastern Air Force Theatre marking around the mid-fuselage and wing tips consisting of a 28" wide yellow band edged with 4" wide black edges. The whole rear fuselage was a replacement section from a 67th FBS Sabre.The aircraft letter 'Q' was 42" high. The national insignia were 30" diameter on the wing upper and lower surfaces. Note the 2 Squadron emblem on the nose.
References used: p.25 *South African Colours and Markings Vol 1 No.4*, by Piet Van Schalkwyk, William Marshall and Stefaan Bouwer, Colour and Markings Books, 2002.

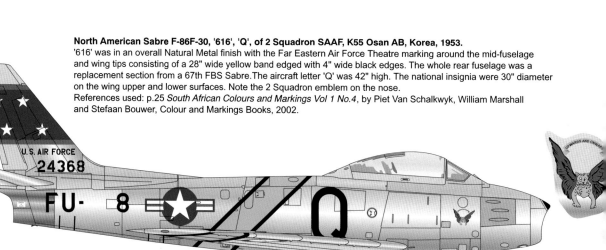

North American Sabre F-86F-30, '616', 'Q', 'LADY of LORETTE' of 2 Squadron, SAAF, K55 Osan AB, Korea, 1953.
This llustration shows '616' some time later in full SAAF markings. Overall Natural Metal finish with the Far Eastern Air Force Theatre markings around the mid-fuselage and wing tips. The aircraft letter 'Q' was 42" high. The national insignia were 30" in diameter on the wing upper and lower surfaces with the fuselage examples being 36" diameter. The fin flash was 84" high and 27" wide.
Note the 2 Squadron emblem on the nose.
References used: p.25 *South African*
Colours and Markings Vol 1 No.4, by Piet Van Schalkwyk, William Marshall and Stefaan Bouwer, Colour and Markings Books, 2002.

Canadair Sabre F.6, '360', 'B', of 2 Squadron, SAAF, early 1960s.
In April 1954, the SAAF bought thirty-four Canadair Sabre F Mk 6s. They carried an overall Natural Metal finish with the yellow and black Far Eastern Air Force Theatre markings overpainted with red around the mid-fuselage and wing tips both 28" wide edged with 4" wide black edges. The red aircraft letter 'B' appears to have been 24" high.
The new SAAF national insignia at this time appear to have been 24" in diameter on the fuselage, wing upper and wing lower surfaces. The fin flash also appears to have been wider - the dimensions unknown. 8" high black fuselage and approximately 28" high underwing serials were carried under both wings. References used: *Canadair Sabre Mk.1-6, Commonwealth Sabre Mk.30-32 in RCAF-RAF-RAAF-SAAF-Luftwaffe & Foreign Service* by Richard Ward, Aircam Books No.20, 1971.

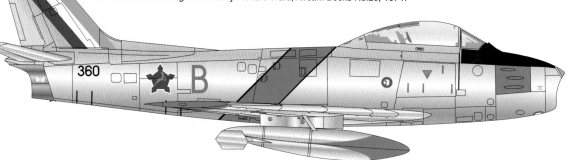

Canadair Sabre F.6, '382', 'P', of 1 Squadron, SAAF, early 1960s.
This SAAF operated Canadair Sabre F Mk 6 wore this overall Natural Metal finish with the yellow and llack Far Eastern Air Force Theatre markings replaced with blue and orange examples around the mid-fuselage consisting of a 28" wide blue band edged with 4" wideorange edges.
The blue aircraft letter 'P' appears to have been 24" high and was also placed on the centreline of the fuselage underside possibly having a height of 40". The SAAF national insignia appears to have been 24" in diameter on the fuselage, wing upper and wing lower surfaces.
The fin flash also appears to have been wider although the dimensions unknown. 8" high black fuselage and approximately 28" high underwing ser were carried under both wings. Areas of Day-Glo Fluorescent Red bands adorn the tailfin, upper and undersurfaces of the tailplanes, rear fuselage roots, wingtips and the nose area. Also note the blue and orange bands on the fuel tanks.
References used: *Private photo archives and Canadair Sabre Mk.1-6, Commonwealth Sabre Mk.30-32 in RCAF-RAF-RAAF-SAAF-Luftwaffe & Foreign Service* by Richard Ward, Aircam Books No.20, 1971.

Above: Canadiar Sabre F.6, '367' of No 2 Squadron, SAAF, early 1960s, seen in the natural metal finish worn during this period. No 2 Squadron carried a red fuselage band, outlined in blue, red wing tips and wing fuel tank markings, again outlined with a thin blue strip. They also carried large red aircraft codes on the rear fuselage. The large colourful Squadron markings are carried on both sides of the nose. The SAAF purchased thirty-four Canadair Sabres in 1954 after the original F-86Fs used in Korea had been returned to the USAF. The last Sabre was phased out of service with the SAAF in 1979 when they were replaced by Mirage IIIs.

Photo: *Adrian Balch Collection*

Above: Canadiar Sabre F.6, '363' of No 1 Squadron, SAAF, circa 1970. This was the final colour scheme worn by the South African Air Force Sabres. The colours were Deep Buff BS381C:360 and Olive Drab BS381C:298 upper surfaces with Light Admiralty Grey BS381C:697 undersides. Unusual for SAAF Sabres, this aircraft did not feature the Squadron badge on fin or nose.

Photo: *Adrian Balch Collection.*

Above: Canadiar Sabre F.6, '377' of No 1 Squadron, SAAF, circa 1960s, seen in the overall natural metal finish worn during the 1960s. The No 1 Squadron badge can be seen on the nose and the blue band on the tanks.

Photo: *Adrian Balch Collection*

Left: Canadiar Sabre F.6, '381' of No 1 Squadron, SAAF, 1960s. The 1 Squadron blue fuselage band and wing tips can be clearly seen in this picture. No 1 Squadron also had blue aircraft code letters. The Squadron badge can also be seen on the nose. Note the open gun bay, drooped air brake and leading edge slats on the wings.

Photo: *Adrian Balch Collection*

Pakistan Air Force (*Pakistan Fiza'ya*)

Pakistan acquired some 120 F-86F-35s under an Mutual Defence Assistance Program, (MDAP), deliveries starting in 1954. Most, if perhaps not all, were re-manufactured airframes with the longer span -40 wings. The type became the main Pakistani fighter of the period and several squadrons operated them, seeing combat action in the Indo-Pakistan War of 1965.

It was at this time that the Indian Air Force was operating Folland Gnat light fighter, and this type took a heavy toll of Pakistani Sabres and F-104s, earning itself the nickname of the 'Sabre Slayer'. It wasn't all one-way however, with Pakistani F-86Fs claiming IAF Hunter 'kills' and even forcing an Indian Gnat to land in Pakistan.

Many Pakistani Sabres were also wired-up and equipped to carry AIM-9B Sidewinder AAMs. Due to the fact that the technology was still in its infancy, these early versions of the AIM-9 were unable to 'see' their targets against the reflected heat emissions from the ground and many 'misfires' were recorded .

When originally delivered, Pakistani Sabres were finished in an overall natural metal scheme, with black anti-glare panels. Colourful tail and nose checkerboards were subsequently applied to many.

In 1966, the PAF took delivery of a further ninety F-86s, this time Canadair Sabre Mk 6s, passed on from the *Luftwaffe*.

In 1971, Pakistan again found itself at war with its larger neighbour to the east, and the Sabres were again in action. By this time however, the IAF was fielding much more potent types such as the MiG-21, so the Sabre found itself increasingly outclassed.

Several Pakistani Sabres found their way into the air force of Bangladesh, where ground crews, with the help of Pakistani defectors, maintained them, until their ultimate replacement by MiG-21s.

Towards the end of their careers, PAF Sabres acquired various

Above: Canadiar Sabre Mk 6, 1756, Pakistani Air Force, The Sabres were originally delivered in this natural metal finish and shows AIM-9 Sidelwinder missiles and fule tanks under each wing. This particular aircraft is preserved in the Pakistani Air Force Museum.
The Sabres entered service with in 1954 and fought in both the both Indo-Pakistan wars. They flew with Nos 14, 17, 18 and 19 Squadrons and finally left Pakistani service in the early 1980s.
Photo: MR Collection

disruptive camouflage schemes of dark green and medium grey upper surfaces over light grey undersides, (possibly ex-Luftwaffe NATO colours?), or plain dark green upper surfaces over light grey undersides.

By the early 1980s, all the Pakistani Sabres had been withdrawn from service. In 1975 some were passed on to Burma.

Canadair Sabre Mk 6, '54987', of the Pakistani Air Force, early 1970s.
Overall Natural Metal finish with black serials on rear fuselage. The Pakistani national insignia diameters appear to have been either 24" or 30" diameter - in all six positions. The fin insignia could possibly have been 24" square.
References used: private photo archives.

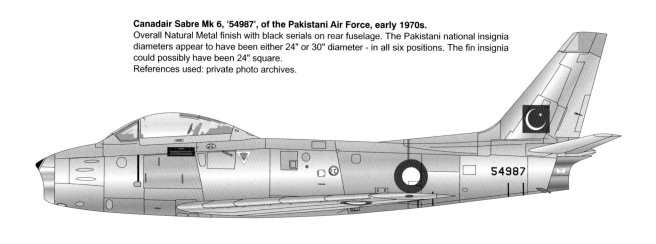

Canadair Sabre Mk 6, '177', of the Pakistani Air Force, mid-1970s.
Upper surface colours comprised dark green and dark grey shades over medium grey shade undersides, which may have been ex-Luftwaffe NATO colours. Black serials on the rear fuselage. The Pakistani national insignia appear to have been either 24" or 30" diameter in all six positions. The fin insignia could possibly have been 24" in square. Note the last three digits of the serial repeated in white on the nose.
References used: private photo archives.

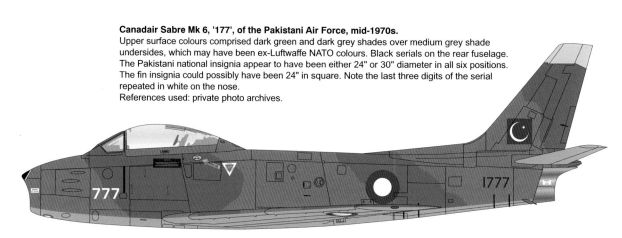

Malaysian Air Force
(Tentara Udara Diraja Malaysia)

The TUDM took delivery of ten ex-Australian Sabre Mk 32s in October 1969, with another eight following two years later, although two of these were not in an airworthy condition. Like other ex-RAAF Sabres, these aircraft were delivered in their original anti-corrosion Aluminium lacquer scheme, but this soon gave way to an overall dark green upper surface scheme, with light grey undersides. The type's use in TUDM service was limited, and by 1976, they had been replaced by the Northrop F-5A. After withdrawal, a few of these were sold to Indonesia, where they served until 1980.

Left: CAC Sabre Mk 27: FM1905, of No 11 Squadron, *Tentara Udare Diraja Malaysian*, (Royal Malaysian Air Force) circa 1970s.

When the RAAF retired their Sabres a number were passed onto the *Tentara Udare Diraja Malaysian*. They were delivered in the original RAAF silver lacquer finish but by the early 1970s they had been repainted in dark green upper surfaces with blue-grey undersides.

The serial was applied in white on the rear fuselage, with the TUDM mid blue, dark blue and yellow National Insignia markings in all six positions and on both sides of the fin. This picture shows a preserved Sabre at Butterworth Air Force Base.

Photo: *MR Collection*

North American (CAC) Sabre Mk 27, 'FM1371', of No 11 Squadron, Tentara Udara Diraja Malaysia, late 1960s.
Overall Aluminium lacquer finish with black anti-glare panel and 8" high serials. Grey fin tip. The Malaysian national insignia were either 24" or 30" square - in all six positions.
The fin flash appears to have been 24" high by 18" wide.
References used: page 95, *Wings of Fame*, Volume 10, Aerospace Publishing, 1989.

North American (CAC) Sabre Mk 27, 'FM1901', of No 11 Squadron, Tentara Udara Diraja Malaysia, early 1970s.
Dark green upper surfaces over blue-gray undersides with black anti-glare panel and pale grey fin tip. White, 10" high, serials on rear fuslage. The Malaysian national insignia were either 24" or 30" square - in all six positions. The fin flash was possibly 30" high by 24" wide. Note the black 'de-icing' strip along the wing leading edges.
References used: private photo archives.

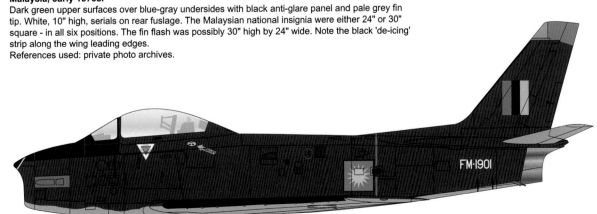

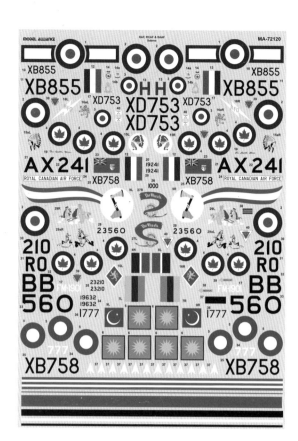

To: The Aviation Workshop   Tel: 01235 769038
Brook Barn, Letcombe Regis   Fax: 01235 771432
Wantage, Oxon OX12 9JD
Email: sales@theaviationworkshop.co.uk

Name...

Address..

....

....

Post Code.....................Country...............................

Tel No:.......................Email:...................................

**Please supply either Telephone Number or Email in case
we need to contact you or there is a problem.**

Please Send be the On-Target Decals F-86 Sabre

☐ MA-72120 1/72 Scale Pt 1 £9.00
☐ MA-48120 1/48 Scale Pt 1 £13.00
☐ MA-72125 1/72 Scale Pt 2 £9.00
☐ MA-48125 1/48 Scale Pt 2 £13.00

Postage: Post Free in UK; Overseas Customers add 20%

☐ I wish to pay by UK Sterling cheque, payable to The
Aviation Workshop

☐ I wish to pay by Credit/Debit Card (Please Tick)

AMERICAN EXPRESS Card ☐   VISA ☐   MasterCard ☐   SWITCH ☐   Switch Valid from: ☐   Issue No. ☐

Card No:

☐☐☐☐ ☐☐☐☐ ☐☐☐☐ ☐☐☐☐   ☐☐☐

Name on card: . . . .

Expiry date: ☐☐ ☐☐

Please enter the last 3 digits on the signiature strip: ☐☐☐
(reverse side of card)